Because it has had such a dramatic impact upon its readers, this book has been translated, printed and distributed in the following languages:

Afrikaans		Portuguese
English		Spanish
German	Norwegian	Swedish

Walking and Leaping is also printed and distributed in:

England	Canada	New Zealand

Books by Merlin Carothers have now been translated and printed into thirty-one languages. Their unique and powerful messages have caused them to be distributed in sixty countries.

By the same author

Prison to Praise
Power in Praise
Answers to Praise
Praise Works!
Bringing Heaven into Hell
Victory on Praise Mountain
The Bible on Praise
More Power to You!

Merlin R. Carothers

Walking & Leaping

edited by
David Manuel, Jr.

MERLIN R. CAROTHERS
ESCONDIDO, CALIFORNIA

to the millions who have read the "praise books"

CONTENTS

CONTENTS

Walking and Leaping

1. A Methodist Preacher in Ambia

"Praise the Lord," I said softly, turning away from the front window and shaking my head in awe. Parked in front of the house, gleaming in the early morning sun, was a brand-new Oldsmobile station wagon, and hitched behind it was an equally new Holiday trailer, capable of sleeping six. In less than an hour, Mary and I, and Joann (20), Bruce (11), and Genie (8) would be taking off on the first vacation I'd had in years. And not for just a fast week crammed into an impossible schedule, but a whole month . . . .

Even that wasn't the biggest thing. We were on our way to southern California, where God had called us to start a new work. He had revealed almost nothing of His plan, beyond clear guidance to Mary and me that that was where

He wanted us. I looked back out the window; the sky was clear, and the dew on the lawn sparkled in the morning sun——a perfect day to start a trip.

"Merlin?" Mary came up behind me. "Do you think we ought to put our coats in the back of the wagon, or in the trailer?"

The Indiana winter of '72 had been long and cold, with an unusual number of below-zero days. But today was the first day of June, and where we were going, we would hardly need winter clothes at all. "Put them in the trailer," I said, grinning. Mary had carefully packed all our most precious belongings there, and she was proud of how much she had been able to get in. She had even assisted a carpenter in the church to put extra storage shelves in an unused corner of the trailer. All at once I was anxious to get going. I took a last look around the bare living room——the movers had loaded our furniture the day before——and went outside to make a final check of the wagon and trailer.

A careful pre-flight inspection is a matter of habit for anyone who has done his own flying, and I went slowly around the wagon and trailer one last time, making sure that the rear end of the wagon was at the right height to carry the big trailer evenly, and checking the heavy-duty trailer hitch which had been expertly installed by one of Lafayette's finest trailer companies. Everything seemed fine, and I looked up at the lovely parish house our people had built for us, just as the front door opened and Mary and the kids came out, their arms loaded with last-minute, remembered necessities.

At that moment a familiar car pulled up. It was Gene and Vivian Leak, two of our dearest friends in the parish I was leaving. Though we'd said goodbye the night before, at an all-stops-out farewell dinner at the church, I was not really surprised to see them. "Couldn't let you take off without anyone to wave, Pastor," Gene said, quietly, and I just put my arm around his shoulder and said nothing.

More cars arrived—more people to wave, more hearts filled with sorrow and joy. Anyone happening to look out his window that morning must have been startled to see the growing number of people laughing and chatting in front of our house at such an early hour. We hated to leave but we had to, and so at length we were all aboard and ready to go. As I turned the key, Gene came over and stuck his head in the window. "Pastor, you know those Monday-night prayer-and-praise meetings at your house?" I nodded. "Well, next Monday's is going to be at our house. And from now on."

"Praise the Lord, Gene," was all I could say.

We left amidst waves and choruses of goodbye, and there wasn't a dry eye in the car or out. Just before I turned the corner of our street, I took a last look in the rear-view mirror at the little cluster of people in front of our house, still waving. I was grateful that our mood soon lapsed into quiet nostalgia. There was a lot I wanted to think about.

My mind went back to the first time I'd met Gene and the others, almost a year before, to the day. After twenty years of being a Methodist chaplain, I had retired as a Lt. Colonel from the Army and reported back to my home conference in central Indiana. I had been led to say nothing to them about my first book, *Prison to Praise,* which had recently become a Christian bestseller, or the just-completed *Power in Praise,* or the requests for speaking engagements that I was beginning to receive. I felt I was to accept without question whatever assignment my church had for me.

And so, at the beginning of summer in 1971, we arrived at the little country town of Ambia—and fell in love with it the moment we got there. Located in the heart of the midwestern farmlands, just east of the Illinois/Indiana border and a couple of hours south-southeast of Chicago, Ambia was so small that many maps don't even show it. The population of the town was only 290, if no one happened to be on vacation. Among other fixtures it boasted a tiny restaurant that closed every afternoon at 6:00, except on weekends, when it didn't open at all, a solitary gas pump that was open if the owner happened to be around to run it and a valiant little post office that was to get quite a work-out on our behalf.

The thing we sensed right away and which grew steadily deeper was that incredible feeling of peace and well-being, for which painters of rural Americana might search all over the nation. The people were mostly farmers; they grew corn and soybeans, and never seemed to hurry or get upset by anything. Neither Mary nor I could believe that such a quiet, restful community actually existed, and after having been stationed all over the world, I for one was ready for exactly what God in His wisdom had picked out for us.

I was actually pastoring two Methodist churches: "the city church," a red-brick, early American building that was said (perhaps with some bias) to be the most beautiful church in the county; and "the country church," a few miles away. Neither of them held more than a hundred people, and regular attendance amounted to about twenty-five souls each. Tucked as far back from the stream of things as they were, they had never heard of the charismatic movement, and again I said nothing of the books I'd written. In fact, it soon became obvious that they had heard little if anything of the simple Gospel message of faith in Christ for salvation.

So that was where we began—with the words of John 3:16: *for God so loved the world that He gave His only begotten Son, that whosoever believeth in Him should not perish, but have everlasting life.* As we lifted up Jesus, and centered on God's love for them and what Christ had done in our lives, it wasn't long before the Lord Jesus became real to them. These were loving, patient, thoughtful people to begin with; when we had arrived they had opened their arms to us beyond anything we had expected, and now that they were discovering that Jesus was the source and the center, their joy knew no bounds.

Jesus saved! Not good works, or good behavior, or rote obedience to the law. Jesus. He did it. Eternal life was His free gift to all who would come unto Him.

As their spirits quickened to this truth, as the light within them began to build, the Enemy could no longer sow his tiny seeds of doubt. Suddenly the whole business of faith began clicking and falling into place. They understood! It was so simple; why had it seemed so hard before? Like the first ride on a two-wheeler, or the first lap across the pool, or the first time down the mountain with both skis together, learning to believe God was something that once they had it, they would have it forever.

For when someone discovers that the Lord is indeed a living, risen Savior, who loves him beyond all comprehension and has been waiting all his life for him to realize it, when he realizes that gaining eternal life does not depend on what he has or hasn't done in the past but only on who Jesus is and what He did, the first thing he usually wants to do is thank and praise the Lord, and the second thing is to tell someone else the Good News. And that's what our people did.

As a result of their enthusiasm, our congregations had doubled by September, and many churches in the immediate area began to offer their pulpits. I accepted these invitations as often as I could, never letting them interfere with my regular Sunday obligations to my own churches and trying to fit them in with my outside speaking engagements. These were now coming in at the rate of six a week. I would try to accept only one or two, to be able to do full justice to my first responsibilities at home, to the "brand-new work" that God was raising up.

And all the while our parishioners never showed any interest in where these out-of-town trips were taking me or what was responsible for the hundreds of letters that were coming through the post office. I was there to preach on

Sunday mornings (there never had been any other meetings) and was available when someone needed to talk privately, and that was enough. And so it might have gone on indefinitely, had not a young couple in our congregation named John and Jenny Scolly taken a trip in September to visit relatives out West. Not surprisingly, their conversation soon turned to their new joy in Christ, and it turned out that their hosts were Christians, too.

"It all began," John explained to them, "when this retired Army chaplain came to be our pastor. Right off, he started preaching about Jesus, and it seemed like that was all he ever did preach about, or even talked about during the week, for that matter, and no one, Methodist or otherwise, had ever heard of the likes of that. But Pastor Carothers is a nice guy, and it wasn't long before some of us tried out what he said, and——"

"Wait a minute!" his host interrupted, "did you say his name is Carothers?"

John nodded, startled at the sudden alertness of his host.

"You don't mean *Merlin* Carothers?" his host said barely audibly.

"Yes, that's him, why? Do you——"

"Don't you know who he is?" and his host jumped out of his chair, grabbed John and took him over to his bookshelf, where there was a stack of *Prison to Praise*. "Here, look at this!"

"So?"

"So that book has changed thousands of lives. John, your pastor's famous!"

"Well, he certainly doesn't seem that way," said John, a little annoyed. "Look, you *sure* it's the same person?"

"Read the book!" was all his host would reply. John did, and several days later he returned to Ambia, with a pile of *Prison to Praise* in the trunk for the rest of the congregation. Instead of going home, he headed straight for the parish house, where he confronted his pastor with the truth.

"How come you've never said anything about this book?" he demanded.

"Why, John," I said seriously, "I'd already taught you everything that was in it anyhow, and I thought it was better that you hear it firsthand than from a book."

"Well, I guess you're right," he said grinning, and hurried off to spread them around the congregation. The next thing I knew he and several others were buying them in quantity and giving them away all over the county. After that, our congregations really began to expand.

That fall, during harvest time, I came to know a depth of joy that I had never experienced before. The love of these people was almost beyond belief. They welcomed us into their homes like members of their family, and baskets containing the pick of their vegetable gardens—corn, tomatoes, beans, peas, the finest vegetables that expert farmers were able to grow—were constantly turning up on our back doorstep.

One golden, sun-drenched afternoon I'll never forget, Mary and I were invited by Gene Leak to go along corn-harvesting. The air was filled with the smell of new-mown hay and the chirping of grasshoppers—exotic treats for us city-folks. We sat in the wagon, bouncing along behind the big thresher that was sending up a solid flow of corn, and laughing like anything as it almost buried us. Up front on the tractor, Gene turned around and shouted, "You two are behaving like a couple of kids on a honeymoon."

By November our congregations had doubled again in size, and enthusiasm had reached a point where the people came to me and asked what I thought about the possibility of having a revival. They said it had been about thirty years since there had been a revival in either the city church or the country church, and the few recent efforts that had been made had been awfully disappointing. They'd tried to have a weekly meeting, and nobody came, and then just a Saturday or Sunday night meeting, but still no one came. But they were willing to try again, and asked me what I thought.

I suggested that we have a one-week meeting and believe that the Lord would supply the people and the means. They agreed and set about spreading the word. The week of the revival came, and it was the coldest weather anyone there could remember. The temperature was down around 20° below zero, and it snowed every night of the meeting. We held the revival at the country church, and the first night 50 hardy souls came to share the Good News. The second night there were about 75, and the remainder of the week the place was jam-packed. Many adults came to accept Christ, and many of their children came right along with them.

Despite the success of the revival, and the now-jubilant mood of the congregation, I didn't introduce the Baptism of the Holy Spirit into the church itself. My superiors in that Methodist conference were not favorably disposed towards the charismatic movement, and it seemed that the Lord would prefer me to remain submitted to their wishes and not jeopardize what was happening in the churches that He had entrusted to me.

However we did initiate a charismatic-type prayer meeting Monday night, in our home, and Mary led a Bible study for the ladies on Tuesday mornings. In the space of half a dozen meetings more than thirty people were appearing every Monday at 8:00 P.M. and often staying till midnight or even later. One after another of these farmers and their wives sought the fullness of the Spirit, and many of them received.

Far from being the divisive element that detractors claim (and thoughtless over-exuberance sometimes provokes), the newly Spirit-filled members of our congregations expressed their joy in love and prayer rather than emotional outbursts. As a result, we were all enriched by their experience.

In January, our people provided us with a new parsonage, designed to contain everything that Mary had ever imagined in a dreamhouse—central heating, which many of the homes in that area did not have, central air-conditioning which was almost unheard of, and the most luxurious appointments that were available. We were overwhelmed. Never had I known such complete love and total acceptance. And as Mary looked around her new surroundings, she said, "Oh, Merlin, it's so beautiful. It would take an act of God to ever get me to leave this place." But an act of God was even then in the works.

By this time *Power in Praise* had joined *Prison to Praise* on the national religious bestseller lists, and more speaking invitations than ever were coming in. I continued to limit my acceptances to no more than two a week, and I took Mary with me as often as possible. Many times we would leave church after a Sunday service and race to O'Hare airport in Chicago, to make a dinner or evening meeting that night a thousand miles away. Or, if it were in the east, and the weather looked like it would hold up, I would rent a plane at Rantoul Air Force Base in Illinois, forty miles away, and we would have the fun of flying ourselves. Sometimes we would run low of gas with a solid cloud cover beneath and no way of telling exactly where we were, or where the nearest field was. But fear was never present in our cockpit. The Lord was using us to spread His message of praise in *all* circumstances, and if we weren't living it first, our spirits could hardly be used as channels through which the Holy Spirit could quicken others.

Nor were we ever late, though sometimes it was close. I remember one time in March of '72, we were due at a Full Gospel Businessmen's dinner of some 500 people at Martinsville, New Jersey, which my publisher, Dan Malachuk, had arranged. We took off from the field in Rantoul in plenty of time, with the prospect of ideal, CAVU conditions (Ceiling Absolute, Visibility Unlimited). But as we crossed the Ohio/Pennsylvania border, heavy weather began to pile up in front of us, till there was no way we could get over, under or around it. We finally had to call it quits at a little strip in Brandywine, Pennsylvania, about two hours from Martinsville. By the time we climbed down from the airplane the weather was so socked in, it was strictly EBAW (Even the Birds Are Walking).

By the time I was able to get to a phone, it was a little after five, and the dinner was scheduled to begin at seven. Dan, bless his heart, sounded completely unruffled, as I explained that I'd rented a car, and we'd be there as fast as possible. The Lord guided our car over unfamiliar, rain-slick roads and we arrived a few minutes after seven. It was only later that I learned that that afternoon, as the hours stretched out with no word from us, Dan was overheard to mutter, "Small planes are not scriptural!"

In all these meetings, whether there were a few dozen, a few hundred, or a few thousand, the people unfolded like flowers in the sun at the message of praise. Back then, many of them had not heard the message before, and were astounded to learn what can happen when one does what the Bible commands in Ephesians 5:20, *"Giving thanks always for all things"* and praising and thanking God *for* the very situation which is causing so much grief or bitterness or despair. It seems impossible that this act of blind, grit-your-teeth-and-do-it obedience could be responsible for miracles, but the act of praising does two things simultaneously: it softens the heart, and it enables the divine machinery to be set into motion on our behalf, machinery that is awesomely powerful, just waiting for the deep change of heart true praise invariably produces. That was my message, that was what my books were about, and the glory was that anyone who tried it could experience it for himself.

Everywhere we went, people would testify to the fantastic results of applying the principle of praise in their lives, and we made friends by the thousands. When I saw how many people were being blessed, and how deeply, I hated to disappoint those requesting speaking engagements. But Mary would remind me that I wasn't the only one who could pass on the good word of praise, that the Lord knew I could only accept so many and He would take care of the rest. All I had to do was to listen to Him carefully, and to make sure that I accepted only those He specifically wanted me to. But I felt such a burden on my heart to get the message of praise as far as possible, I would tell Him over and over that in all my life this was the thing I wanted most: to reach as many people as possible with the revelation He had given me.

In addition to one-evening commitments, I was also receiving a number of requests for three and four-day missions. One of these, for a full five days, arrived from a town in southern California I'd never heard of, named Escondido, from a pastor I had never heard of, named Vernon Gortner.

There were several reasons why, in the natural, I would not have considered it: it would mean having to be away

Sunday, and in the ten months I'd been in Ambia, that had only happened once; and this was not a church but something which Pastor Gortner referred to as the 120 Fellowship——after the 120 believers who had received the fullness of the Spirit on the Day of Pentecost. It sounded a little far out. I normally would have declined the request in favor of two of the other invitations that came in for the same week in April.

But increasingly in the last few years the Lord had been teaching me that I was to obey His guidance without question. I still questioned Him too often, but I was learning to trust Him more and more. Praise, which is a spoken expression of trust, seems to build trust, and the more one trusts Him, the easier it is to praise. With trust also comes patience: if you don't hear the Lord clearly in a given decision, wait until you do. There's no telling what He'll do in the meantime.

But there was no need to wait in connection with Pastor Gortner's invitation; seldom had I had such a strong indication in my heart that this was one appointment I was to keep, and that Mary was to come, too. So before we really knew what was happening, we were stepping off the plane in San Diego, into weather that was a balmy forty degrees warmer than what we'd left in Chicago.

Our first meeting in Escondido was in the regular location of the 120 Fellowship, an old frame building called the Women's Club. Pastor Gortner had been holding meetings there for the past four years as the Lord raised up a core of Spirit-filled believers, who met regularly on Thursday nights and maintained their involvement in their own individual churches. The Women's Club, bulging slightly, seated approximately 200 people. That night, some 500 people were shoe-horned into every available cranny, even hanging out the windows——people who had driven from all over southern California to hear the message of praise.

From there I went to the San Diego chapter of the Full Gospel Business Men's Fellowship and spoke at a dinner in the banquet hall of one of the large hotels there, to 800 people, the largest attendance they'd had in their history. From there I went to a Baptist church in Los Angeles, at which every square foot was occupied by someone sitting, kneeling or standing. Then it was back to Escondido for one more meeting with the 120 Fellowship.

Throughout our stay people kept coming up to us and urging us to come back to Escondido and establish an inter-denominational work of some kind. The most enthusiastic of these was our host, Pastor Gortner himself. Every chance he had he would say something like, "Now you've really got to admit that you've never seen country so breathtakingly beautiful," and laughing we would admit we hadn't. Or, "Have you noticed that the weather has been perfect every day that you've been here? I imagine you're wondering if it ever *does* rain around here. Well it does, just enough to grow the sweetest oranges and grapefruit you've ever set your lips to." "You mean, it got that cold? And stayed that cold? No wonder so many Indiana farmers take winter vacations down here!" Again we would laugh and point out that nearly everywhere we went people would urge us to come and stay. But neither of us had ever been so happy as we'd been in Ambia, and the Lord had never given any indication that He intended to move us.

On a few occasions Vernon would wax serious. He would speak of the vision that God had given him, of a major, inter-denomination, charismatic Christian center in the Escondido area, and of the hunger of the people who lived in those parts for a deeper walk in the Spirit. He would close by simply asking us to keep the possibility open before the Lord. We assured him we would, but it wasn't until the last day that Mary and I even mentioned it to each other.

On that warm and sparkling day we had a little time to ourselves, so we went out by the pool of the Mt. Vernon Motel where we were staying, and sat down on the diving board. No one else was there at the time, and diamonds of sunlight danced and shimmered on the smooth surface of the water. We watched them for awhile without speaking, then Mary said, "Merlin, wouldn't it be something if God did . . . "

Her voice trailed off, but I knew what she was thinking. I nodded and also knew that I could never be certain that it wasn't my own flesh luring me with all the heady beauty this little corner of the world had to offer. But I also knew that just because a place was beautiful did not mean that God could never give it to His children. We said little more at that time, other than to agree to hold the possibility open before the Lord.

Once again, in the natural, it made no sense at all. The place was too beautiful. There was no poverty, no real suffering observable in the people, and I had always thought that if the Lord ever did call us out of our small community life, it would be to slum work in some major metropolis. I must confess I dreaded that possibility, because I felt so completely inadequate to help anyone. But that was the thought in my mind. As we'd been to Chicago for meetings more than 25 times, I had decided that would probably be the place, as the need was so great.

Another consideration was that if it was to be a work of any size, it would have to be in a big city. Escondido was tucked away from everything——the name itself meant "hidden valley"——and had a population of 40,000 with 30 well-established churches and undoubtedly many more less well known. There was no source of people from which to draw, without sheep-stealing, and I knew that was not God's way. No, rationally, logically, it made no sense.

In any event, it was impossible for me to hear the Lord clearly in such beautiful surroundings, and I resolved to wait until I got back to Indiana, to get alone with Him and wait upon His leading, if any. Mary, I learned later, was thinking along similar lines. The Lord had given her the house of her dreams and surrounded her with love. He would have to do a deep work in her heart for her to completely be at peace about leaving it, though she would go wherever He wanted her.

But just being home again did not miraculously clarify the situation; on the contrary, my mind was more agitated than ever. Now all the natural advantages of my present circumstances, to say nothing of the blessings God had bestowed, impressed themselves upon me. Aside from the immediate security of two growing churches, a delightful parsonage and a congregation unstinting in its love and support, all of which were mine as long as I wanted to stay, I saw the security of retirement that the Methodist Church offered. I was 47 and logically it seemed right that I should give some thought to the future and providing for my family. The retirement program of the Methodist Church, coupled with my benefits as a retired Lt. Colonel, assured that our needs for the rest of our lives would be amply provided for.

Besides which, despite the entrenched antagonism my superiors felt towards the charismatic experience and the extreme unlikelihood that I would be permitted full freedom of worship in my churches, I had a real sense of loyalty to and an affection for the Methodist church. I *was* a Methodist minister, and had never thought of myself as anything but.

Was I supposed to give up all this to go to a community where there was no established church, no home, no income, and not the slightest assurance of what the future might hold, if, indeed, it held anything? It made no sense whatsoever. Around and around my mind went, until in desperation I spent a week in prayer and fasting. I trusted Him, but I would have to be absolutely certain I was hearing Him correctly.

I begged the Lord to pull the cobwebs out of my head and

my heart and deal with my turbulent emotions. I knew that the anxiety I was experiencing was unbelief, and I asked Him to forgive me and show the way. But sometimes, to build our faith, the Lord will refrain from immediately offering red-light/green-light guidance. And this seemed to be such a case. I sensed that it would be well within His permissive will for us to stay right where we were and simply carry on as we had been, but that He might be waiting to see if we were willing to take a fairly large step of blind faith towards the center of His perfect will for us.

In the end I decided to do something I had not done in years: I decided that, like Gideon, I would put out a fleece, the hardest that I could conceive of. If the Lord wanted us to go to California, He would have to: 1, give the witness to the hearts of the flock I had grown to love so strongly and provide them with the right pastor to take my place; 2, open up the way for all our considerable furniture and belongings to be shipped to California, for we could never afford to do it ourselves, and I knew that the believers out there did not have the wherewithal, either; and 3, give both Mary and me absolute peace in our hearts about leaving and the certainty that this was, indeed, His highest will for us.

No sooner had I made these conditions than I knew peace of mind for the first time in what seemed like months. It was in His hands now, and while the conditions seemed impossible, I knew that in Him nothing was impossible. But there were a few things I had to do on my part. So I got in touch with my District Superintendent to tell him that I was considering a call to a new work in California. The first thing he told me was that they were having a very hard time finding pastors to fill all the churches they had open. Normally, he said, it would be months before they could find a replacement for me. On my end of the phone I nodded, relieved to be able to set California aside and get back to practical day-to-day concerns. *But,* the District Superintendent went on, it happened that by an apparently extraordinary coincidence they had just received a request from a bright young fellow (a bit evangelical for their tastes, I gathered from his inferences) who was looking for a small country parish in Indiana, which sounded exactly like the one I was in.

"All right, Lord, that's half of the first one." But I was grinning as I said it.

The next thing that happened, I overheard someone say that they had recently taken advantage of a military retirement benefit that I had never heard of, and had all their personal effects transferred at government expense. "You mean to say, that even after your retirement you're still entitled to one complete move?" I couldn't believe it, but a call to the military confirmed that they were ready to move me anywhere within the continental United States. "Okay, Lord, that's number two."

By this time I felt I had to share my concern with some of our closest friends. "Pastor," Gene Leak said, smiling one Monday night in our living room, "we knew that God had something special in mind for you, and it was only a matter of time before He let you in on it. We're just grateful that He brought you here to get us started." I turned away so that he could not see my eyes filling.

That night, after the others had left, Mary said, "I have peace, Merlin: I love these people, and I love what the Lord has given us here. But I can leave now without any tearing in my heart." And in my own heart I felt the same.

When I awoke the following morning, I knew we were going. So I called Vernon and told him, and he just laughed and said that in the past week three people had come up to him, bubbling over with excitement, to tell him the Lord had told them I was coming.

And then I had the most difficult thing of all to do, and I determined to do it that very Sunday. The church was full to the brim, as all our services were now, but as the last strains of the offertory died away and people settled back for the sermon, only a few suspected what I was about to say.

"My dear friends, I——" And my voice broke, and I started to weep. Somehow, I got out that the Lord was leading me to leave and it was all I could do to get even the bare minimum said, for they were weeping, too.

The next day we began making preparations, and again things went much more quickly and smoothly than we would have thought possible. June 1, less than two weeks away, was to be our departure date. The movers were scheduled, the Lord provided a beautiful new station wagon and trailer, and suddenly it was the evening of May 30th, and the congregation was giving us a farewell banquet in the basement of the church.

It was a splendid affair! The women in these parts were renowned to be the best cooks in central Indiana, and that night they were determined to outdo themselves. Salads, pastries, meat dishes, casseroles—the buffet was beyond belief, and I could imagine the chef of the Waldorf Astoria green with envy.

As the evening progressed, I rejoiced in my heart as one after another shared that they were convinced this was what the Lord wanted for us. I was astonished at how many people came up and quietly gave us money with strict instructions not to save it but to spend it at the Grand Canyon or Yosemite or wherever their own favorite vacation spots were. The Lord had not only provided the longest vacation I'd ever had; He had assured that it would be wholly paid for.

But the high point of the evening for us came when a number present felt led to stand up and share what the message of praise had meant in their lives.

I'll never forget the testimony of one good farmer, who was not a man for many words. It was a miracle in itself that he was standing before a large group testifying. All his life he had a severe back problem which greatly hampered the work he had to do and caused him almost constant pain.

"All right," He said, out loud, "if Pastor Carothers says that God heals, then I am going to start praying and praising. And I did, right there in the barnyard. Chickens must have thought I'd gone plumb loco. And I kept it up, on and off, for several days. I think my wife," and he glanced in her direction, "thought I'd gone plumb loco. Anyway, I was on my tractor one afternoon, when all of a sudden, for the first time in my life, I felt the Lord speaking to me. Now I'm not saying I *heard* anything, but inside He was telling me something, and I knew it was Him, and not just me fooling myself." He paused and looked around the room, to see if there were any doubters. Though we were grinning, we were hanging onto every word.

"He was telling me I was healed. Just like that. And I believed Him. And I was." He sat down then, as abruptly as he'd gotten up, and we all joined in spontaneous praising the Lord . . . .

"Praise the Lord," I cried jubilantly, startling Mary and the kids, as we joined up with Interstate 74 and pointed the nose of the wagon west.

2. Miracles Along the Way

Wagon west—it sounded like a wagon-master's cry. I could just imagine us a century earlier, one of a long line of prairie schooners stretched out for half a mile or so over the vast open terrain, maybe over the very trail we were following. I could almost hear the whistle and crack of the whips and the "Hyah!" of the drivers, as they encouraged their oxen, the creaking of the big wheels and the jingling of pots, pans and paraphernalia hanging in back. The lush green scenery rolled by, alternating with yellow cornfields that stretched to the horizon. Above were sun-dazzled silver clouds in a high, cobblestoned formation. My heart filled with joy. "Hallelujah!" I shouted, and this time the others laughed and joined in. We sang and clapped and praised God at the top of our lungs.

Repeatedly throughout the remainder of that day and the beginning of the next, our hearts could not contain their joy, and we would burst into praise, once within earshot of the restaurant where we had breakfast. But we were so happy that the stares of the folks there were soon followed by smiles. Illinois blended into Iowa, and again the Lord blessed us with glorious weather.

We were rolling down Interstate 80 at the speed limit, Joann and Genie were dozing in the way-back, Bruce was in the back seat and I was up front. Mary was driving and I was poring over the road-maps to see where we would stop for the night. That was the moment Satan chose to reach out and touch the trailer hitch.

Immediately the trailer began to yaw from side to side, forcing the wagon to swerve violently back and forth across the three-lane highway. Tires screamed and we narrowly missed cars on either side of us. Desperately I grabbed the wheel to try to help Mary but both of us with all our might could do nothing as the trailer's yawing rapidly built up momentum and began to lift the front wheels of the wagon clear off the road.

I turned to look at the massive form of the trailer bucking and heaving, just as the wheels on the right side finally collapsed. With a grinding and tearing of metal the trailer went into a roll, and the wagon with it. Across the highway we rolled, over and over, plunging down an embankment alongside. As we were tumbled about the interior of that wagon (never again would we go out of the driveway without having seatbelts buckled), an absolutely incredible peace came over me, and the one thought I had was: "Lord, You must have something really beautiful in mind for us, and I praise and thank You for it."

It was almost an involuntary act on my part. I had no idea where we were going, no sense of direction, as sky, road and grass whirled in front of us. We were falling and flopping around inside like rag dolls.

We landed with a whump, right side up as it happened, and suddenly everything was very still. I can remember thinking, well, thank You, Lord, it looks like You've decided to keep me down here for awhile. I looked over at Mary and knew that she, too, was all right even before she could say so. And the same with the kids. No bones were broken, no flesh was torn, none of us were even scratched. It was unquestionably the greatest personal miracle any of us had ever experienced.

Then I heard a soft hissing noise. The bottled gas tank had come loose from the trailer and was pouring gas out over the car. Lord, if You don't get us out of here quickly, fire could do what the accident couldn't! I tried my door, but it was jammed shut. "Jesus help me," I muttered and smashed my feet against it, springing it open.

Soon, we were clear of the wreckage, standing there and just looking at it in awe. The wagon was totally demolished, and the trailer was nothing but a twisted chassis. Pieces of metal, wood, clothing and belongings were strewn all down the side of the scarred embankment. Mary and I hung on each other, laughing and shaking our heads and saying over and over, "Thank You, Lord! Praise You, Lord!"

"Yes," came a voice behind us, "you folks certainly have a lot to be thankful for. Not one of you should have come out of that mess alive." We turned and looked at an Iowa State Policeman, who was looking at us closely for signs of shock, the more so as we went on praising God. But we deeply appreciated his kindness and courtesy as he took Mary and the children off to the hospital to be checked over, while I stayed behind to wait for the wrecker.

While I was waiting, I looked over the hillside to retrieve what I could of our personal belongings. There wasn't much to be found, but I gathered it up and put it in the trunk of a second police cruiser that was standing by. Just before the tow-truck arrived I took one last look. To my utter amazement, I found the cut crystal cake dish that was Mary's most treasured possession. It was sitting on the ground in the middle of the debris, next to a heavy waffle iron that had been destroyed. It was not even scratched. I felt like waving up at the sky. Of all the things we owned, it was the one thing she would have wanted the most not to lose.

When the wrecker arrived, he asked me what I wanted done. I just told him to do whatever he thought best. I left then with the policeman and joined my family at the Des Moines hospital, where they inspected me. Neither the doctors nor the police could believe that there wasn't so much as a scratch on any of us. We knew more than ever before that God was in control.

I took my family to a motel, and as soon as we were registered, I gathered them all in our room to join in prayer.

We thanked God for preserving each one of us, and thanked Him for the accident, too. At that, Joann, our oldest, who had not yet really learned to praise God, balked.

"I'm sorry, Dad," she said angrily, "but frankly I think you're nuts! Thanking God for that mess out there——that mess that's just everything we own!" And she fought to hold back her tears. "And here we are, the car is gone, our vacation is ruined, and we're stuck in the middle of no-where. And you're praising God? I just don't believe you're real!"

I put my arm around her. "Joann, you wait and see. I have a feeling that God permitted that accident for a very special reason. Maybe just to show you what happens when people will praise Him when they least feel like it." She tried to smile, and buried her head in my shoulder. "Oh, Dad, I really love you, but you know you really are too much."

The first thing next morning, I had a nudge to get out my briefcase and go through it. As I did, a card fell out. On it was the only address I had brought of anyone between the middle of Iowa, and California. The woman's name was Lee Corn, and she lived at Jackson Hole, Wyoming, about a day's travel away. We hadn't planned on stopping so soon, but now, after the accident, it seemed like a good idea. I decided to give her a call.

"Mrs. Corn, this is Merlin Carothers. My family and I are in Iowa, on vacation, heading for the coast. I received your letter and for a reason I don't even know, I have your address with me . . . . "

I could go no further, for the voice at the other end of the line had broken down into uncontrollable sobs. In between I could hear her praising the Lord and asking Him to forgive her for ever doubting. I didn't know what to make of that, so I just prayed for her and waited.

At length she calmed down and tried to explain her reaction. She had just returned from the hospital where she had been receiving cobalt treatments for cancer. The disease had permeated her body and the doctor said that she had no more than a few weeks to live. Someone had given her a copy of *Prison to Praise,* and when the phone rang, she'd been sitting at the dining room table, trying to praise God. But the pain was so great, she didn't know if she was going to be able to make it through the day, much less praise Him. And then she answered the phone and here, she broke down again.

Again, I waited, but all she was able to do was tell me how happy she was that we were coming and that my call and pending arrival were an answer to prayer, the likes of which she'd never heard of, not even in the book. But she would tell me all about it when I got there. I told her I had no idea when that would be, as we were without transportation but I trusted that it wouldn't be too long.

Then God moved so fast it made my head spin. I called my insurance company in Texas, to find out what help they could give us. It turned out they had an agent right there in Des Moines. In a short while there he was, in the flesh. I went with the agent to the wrecker's garage to see the car. He took one look and drove to the Oldsmobile dealer, and asked him if there was any chance of coming near to the model we had had. The dealer smiled and said, "You're not going to believe this." He ushered us into the service area, where they had just finished preparing a wagon that looked to be the literal resurrection of our station wagon. He was right, I couldn't believe it, except that I had a hunch that God was smiling pretty wide.

With the insurance money, this one cost hardly anything, and they filled out the papers on the spot. Next, the insurance agent offered to replace the trailer, but I allowed as how maybe we could make do without a trailer, so he reimbursed us the full amount in cash.

I couldn't wait to see Joann's face. When I pulled into the motel and shared the good news, all she did was shake her head and say, "Oh, wow," over and over.

That same day we were back on the road, looking forward to our interim destination and whatever God might have in store for us. And all in less than 24 hours after our accident. Again, we praised the Lord, and this time there were five voices raised in worship.

It had been dark for some time when we pulled in the drive to the Corn ranch. We had called ahead to let them know we were coming and get final instructions, and all the lights seemed to be on when we arrived. Lee came out to greet us. It was hard to believe that this radiant young mother of only thirty years had any affliction at all, let alone one that was apparently about to take her life. In just a few moments we realized that we were in the home of one of God's most beloved and cherished children.

Her husband Walt was a gruff, hardbitten rancher, who made his living taking people on pack-trips up into the mountains. Walt was polite but aloof, and it was obvious that he was on his best behavior simply because our visit meant so much to the woman he so openly adored. As soon as he graciously could, he excused himself. After showing our kids to bed, he retired himself, and left Lee and Mary and me to carry on about the Lord as long as we liked.

Lee was so full of joy and thanksgiving that sleep was the furthest thing from her mind. In the presence of her enthusiasm any weariness of our own was soon forgotten; in fact, Mary and I both loved her so much, we felt as if we'd known her for years.

That night and the following, she confided to us that the deepest desire of her heart was for Walt to come to know Christ before she died. This she had revealed to her prayer group — several ladies who, like herself, were reaching out for a deeper spiritual walk. It was through them that she had received my book. None of them, Lee said, actually knew of anyone who had been healed by prayer, but they had read about it, and decided to agree in prayer that God would somehow bring me to Jackson Hole, Wyoming. They felt that if I did come, God would use me to do some very important things in their lives. One such thing, Lee believed, was that if I were to come and pray for her, God would grant her heart's desire and save Walt. "And so," she laughed, "that was the reason why, on the one hand, I was so surprised and delighted when you called, but on the other hand, I really wasn't surprised at all!"

That night in the cool mountain air, we slept like logs. It seemed that scarcely an hour had passed when I awoke to hear Lee in the kitchen, humming softly and preparing breakfast. Outside the sun was high and poking an impatient finger through a place where the window shade did not quite close it out. I yawned heavily and tried to bring my wristwatch into focus: 9:00 o'clock. I thanked the Lord for letting us sleep so late, and got up as quietly as I could to keep from waking Mary. No use. And I reminded myself that I should give up ever thinking I could get up without waking her.

Later that morning, I could tell that Walt was seeking some way to show his gratitude for our coming and the tremendous lift it seemed to be for Lee. He asked me how would I like to take a pack-trip on horseback up into the Grand Tetons. I replied with great joy that I had dreamed all my life of taking such a trip, and how much I had enjoyed seeing the Grand Tetons the evening before, as we'd approached.

I asked how much it cost to take such a trip. Because I knew that this was his livelihood I intended to pay the full price. "It would cost $80.00 a day," he said, "but I'm not going to charge you anything. I'd just like to do it for you."

I started to object but got a check in my spirit and accepted with gratitude. "There's just one thing, Walt; I don't see how I could go without Mary. We try to do everything together."

"Well, I'll take her, too."

I got another nudge, and in obedience I had to speak

again. "Walt, there's something else: this is our vacation, the first real one we've had that we've been able to take the kids along. The older two would really be disappointed if we left them behind."

"Well, I'll take all of you."

So Walt began to make plans to take us up into the mountains. He alerted his trail cook and handyman and told them to get ready as quickly as possible for an unscheduled trip. It took two days to get the equipment all ready, and we spent those days with Lee. She took us around to meet her prayer partners, and other Christian friends, and we found them as open and enthusiastic as she was. Every place we went they asked when I was going to talk to them. We decided that they could go ahead and announce a meeting at one of their homes, and we scheduled it for the same night that we would return from our pack-trip.

"Merlin," said Lee, as we headed home that afternoon, "I'll be praying the whole time you're on the trip that the Lord will open up just the right opportunity for you to speak to Walt." I nodded, and she looked out the car window, and bit her lip. "I'm afraid he's what you would call, Gospel-hardened. I may have pushed a bit when I first came to know Jesus, or he just figures he doesn't need the Lord." She sniffed and went on. "Walt's so proud of his self-reliance. My illness is the first thing I've seen get to him."

We turned in the drive, and she made a determined effort to regain her cheerfulness. "Well, as I say, a lot of people have tried to convert him, even ministers. And he's proud that they haven't had any effect on him. But I'll be praying," she said brightly.

In the house, Joann and Bruce were as excited about the now imminent trip as I was, and Mary, who had only been on a horse a couple of times in her life, was praising the Lord.

"Now, you all had better get to bed early tonight," Walt said after dinner. "In fact, you better all get all the rest you can, 'cause you're going to need it."

"Praise the Lord," I heard Mary murmur.

3. God's Country—God's People

The alarm went off at 5:00 the next morning. This time there was no friendly shaft of sunlight poking in around the shade; rosy-fingered dawn was not to make its appearance for another hour or so. It was essential that we set out as early as possible, because we had a lot of ground to cover to reach our base camp high up in the mountains.

"Mount up," called Walt, almost as soon as we stepped out the door. And there stood six mounts and three pack-horses stamping their feet. Their nostrils steamed in the crisp pre-dawn air. Joann, who was an accomplished horsewoman, fairly glided into the saddle, and I managed well enough, as did Bruce who needed only a hand up. But poor Mary needed help getting into the saddle, and I thanked the Lord for giving Walt the insight to pick his most gentle mare for her.

So we started up, Walt was in the lead of course, followed by three pack-horses, then Bruce, me, Mary, Joann, and, bringing up the rear to make sure none of us got lost, the cook and handyman. Up we went. And up and up and up.

The first hour we thoroughly enjoyed the excitement of being on a mountain trail, smelling the fresh woods-smells, listening to the hoofbeats, and craning to look back at the valley and the house that we had started from. As we went over the first mountain ridge, going down for a short spell before starting up again, we began to see new horizons, fifty and a hundred miles away.

Most memorable of all was when Walt suddenly raised his hand. We all stopped and looked where he was pointing. Scarcely a hundred yards away a huge herd of elk, too many to count, was grazing on a grassy slope. We stayed as still as we could, not daring to breathe. But they looked right at us and went on feeding unconcernedly, either sensing that we meant them no harm, or simply never having learned to fear man. All at once one of them got it in mind to take off, and almost as one the rest were in motion, too. They ran together, like a flowing grey river, and in tremendous, continuous, unbelievably graceful leaps, cleared fallen trees, boulders, or anything in their path. They ran so silently, that, when they were gone, and the slope was empty, we almost wondered if we hadn't imagined them.

We also saw deer and coyotes, but after the first hour, we were more concerned with the alarming discovery that our saddles seemed to be getting rougher and rougher.

Our seats, used to nothing harder than the front seat of a car or the living room sofa, began to feel increasingly sensitive. A few more hours, which seemed a day long each, and we reached a beautiful, grassy valley, with a stream of mountain water burbling over the rocks in the sunlight. Walt again raised his hand, and we dismounted, none of us gracefully. Practically all of us needed more than a little assistance.

As Mary and I stood there, looking down at the clearest water I'd ever seen, she leaned over and whispered to me, "Merlin, I'm thirsty." I looked back at the pack-horses and our own, and noticed that there were no canteens on any of them. I was embarrassed to say anything, but by now it had grown quite warm, and we were exhausted. I finally went over and said, "Walt, we're thirsty."

He was inspecting a shoe on one of the horses and looked up, surprised. "Well, go over there and get a drink."

"Drink what," I said, sounding stupid and not caring.

"The stream water."

"Walt, we can't drink that water," I said, thinking of twenty years of Army training and carrying water purification tablets.

"Just drink the water," he said, trying not to sound impatient with the tenderfoot in front of him. "I've been drinking it for years. It's pure," he added pointedly, "just the way God made it."

Well with all sorts of visions of strange diseases and organic malfunctions, I went over, lay down by the bank and put my head down to the water. I had to admit it certainly was beautiful water—— it was almost like it was laughing and happy.

I took a deep breath, put my face into it and drank——of the coolest, sweetest, most delicious water I'd ever tasted. Oh, wow, to quote Joann. I drank till I nearly suffocated. Up came my head, and I startled the nearest horse as I yelled for Mary to come over. She did, and her reaction was the same.

Lunch (for that was what we'd stopped for, though I had hoped it just might be for the night) was simple trail fare ——ham sandwiches, apples, and candy bars——but they tasted like manna from heaven. After lunch, I was just resting my eyes a bit, when Walt's cry of "Mount up!" rang out in the early afternoon air. That wasn't easy, but somehow we managed and soon we were making our way upwards again.

About three o'clock in the afternoon, we came to a snow belt. Deep drifts piled across the trail, and for the first time since we had set out, we began praying in earnest. I looked back at Mary and Bruce who were praying in the Spirit. The snow came up higher and higher, till it began to brush the horses' bellies. I wondered how they would ever find their footing if it got any deeper. (As it later turned out, Walt was wondering, too, and more concerned than any of us. He alone knew that if they couldn't go forward there was no way they were going to get turned around to go back.)

But we made it, and not long after we reached a lovely hidden plateau where we stopped to let the horses rest.

Walt wheeled back and said to Mary, "Well, cheer up, it's not long now; another three hours will see us there."

Mary said later that she would have fainted, if she could have fallen off her horse. But Walt took pity on her and admitted he was just kidding; we had reached our intended campsite. Even so, Mary could not move her legs and had to be lifted out of the saddle, as she whispered "Thank you, Jesus." All of us eastern city-folks had never in our lives been so completely tired and sore. But Walt soon had a big, cheerful campfire going. He unrolled Mary and the kids' sleeping bags right around it, so they could get in them and eat their supper in cozy comfort.

Supper was fried chicken and fresh-baked sourdough biscuits. It is impossible to describe how good it tasted. Soon we were laughing at our bruises and everything was once again right with the world. For dessert there was rich steaming hot cocoa. How good it tasted in that chill mountain night.

Soon all my family was asleep. Later, we would get them up and move them into the tents that had been pitched, back away from the fire, but for now we let them doze. Walt and I sat and gazed into the fire.

"How come you're not like them other preachers?" Walt said at length, without turning from the fire.

"What do you mean, Walt?" I said, not looking up, either.

"Well, you've never tried to convert me, for one thing, and you always seem to be laughing, for another. Even when your tail must have felt like it had been through a tannery, if you'll pardon the expression."

41

"Well, Walt, that's what happens when you've got Jesus inside of you. He changes the way you look at things. Because He changes what you are, way down inside."

Walt poked a stick at a log that needed turning. "Well, I kind of thought I'd like to change—you know, on the inside, like you said——particularly for Lee, after she got so excited about this Christian thing. I tried real hard, too. A couple of times. But it wasn't any good. In three days I was my old self again." He cleared his throat and thought a bit, while I just listened. And waited.

He gave a deep sigh and said in a voice I could barely make out, "I'm not good enough to ever be a Christian, that's for sure," and he chucked the stick he held into the fire.

"That's where you're wrong, Walt," I said softly. "But I'll tell you where I've heard that before: over in Vietnam. Too many times. The Med-Evac choppers would land at the combat hospital and medics would bring in these young, teen-age kids. They were torn up so bad, there was no point in the doctors even kidding them about their having any chance to live." Walt looked at me, but I didn't look up. "I would try to tell those boys that it didn't matter what they'd done or what they were like inside. Salvation was a free gift. It was for anyone who would accept Jesus as his Lord and Saviour."

I looked up then. "Do you know, one boy—he couldn't have been more than seventeen—with what was almost his dying breath tried to argue with me and tell me I was wrong?" Walt shook his head. "I carried a Bible with me, and I showed it to him, in John 3:16, and I John 1:9. Nothing he did or didn't do would have any effect on his going to heaven, once he had confessed his sins before the Lord and asked Jesus to forgive him and come into his heart."

Walt rested his chin on his fist and stared at me. "Well, I got that boy to see the truth," I went on, "and he broke down and asked Jesus to cleanse him of his sins and take him home. And then he died. In my arms."

Walt's eyes were full, but he didn't turn away. "But you know, he didn't die, not really. Oh, sure, his body did. But his soul went on to live forever, with the One who came to give eternal life."

I looked at Walt. "Would you like to accept Jesus now?" And he nodded, tears streaming down his cheeks.

We were awakened the next morning by a thunderous, "Praise the Lord, Merlin and Mary, it's time to get up!" right outside our tent. Mary's eyes sprang open. "Was that—" I nodded. "Did he say—" I nodded again. "Well, praise the Lord yourself!" Mary called out joyously.

Getting dressed without getting out of the warmth of one's sleeping bag was an art I had clearly not mastered, even though I had tried a thousand times during four wars. My contortions caused Mary to explode with mirth. This made me all the more determined, and as I tussled with my left sock, rolling this way and that, I nearly brought down the tent.

"Hey, Merlin, you got a *bear* in there?" Walt was irrepressible this morning.

But the clink of tin cups, the clank of frying pans, and the aroma of frying bacon and eggs, was too much. I gave up, got out, got dressed, and emerged sheepishly from the tent, to an entirely unnecessary round of applause.

We looked out over the valley and saw the horses that Walt had hobbled the night before grazing contentedly what seemed like almost a mile away. Walt's own horse was tethered close by, and he would shortly ride out and bring the others in. What he had done the night before was wrap a strap of leather around each horse's forelegs, giving them the freedom to hop to wherever they chose to forage, but not to run. Walt told us that it was difficult to train horses to take a hobble and some never did, but once they did it was by far the best way to insure they get adequate grazing during the night.

Our appetites that morning astounded us. City folk like us usually don't even know if we want to eat breakfast or just skip it. That morning we could have eaten a whole cow. As it was we polished off enormous quantities of bacon, eggs, biscuits and peaches, and washed it down with fresh-perked coffee.

Inevitably it came time to climb back up into the saddle, but with uncharacteristic compassion——in fact, for him, downright tenderness——Walt passed on some very welcome trail lore: our muscles would gradually loosen up today, and by tomorrow we would be so comfortable in the saddle, we'd be ready to go another week. We found that hard to believe, but decided to take it on faith. In the meantime we wondered what we were going to do about the rest of today.

Walt then set another precedent, informing us of our objective beforehand (Hidden Lake), when we could expect to get there (around lunchtime), and our final destination (back to our present camp).

Sure enough, around noon, we arrived at Hidden Lake. It was like a dream. It was crystal clear, about a hundred yards across, and you could see right to the bottom. As we stood there, two large white birds as big as swans and not unlike them came in, flaps down, for perfect landings at the far end of the lake. Walt said of this particular species that they would not tolerate another pair of birds on any lake and a vicious fight would ensue if any others showed up.

We had lunch and were peacefully lounging by the edge of the lake, when Walt asked me if I would like to do a little fishing. Well, old perceptive Merlin didn't notice any fishing poles anywhere, so I steeled myself for another gag. Instead Walt pulled a box out of his saddle bag, opened it and quickly assembled a full-fledged, fly-fishing rod and reel. Selecting a fly from the box and attaching it, he handed the rig to me and said, "Now do a good job; you're responsible for providing our breakfast for tomorrow morning."

I thanked God that I had used a fly rod before and knew how to feed the line out gradually. I kept it flicking back and forth in the air in longer and longer arcs. When I had about as much line out as I could manage, I attempted to sail the line out to its fullest extent and watched it settle on the surface of the water, not all that far away. Chagrined, I hastened to reel it in but had only gotten a turn or two on the reel when *ping*——the line tautened. Out of the water leaped a beautiful mountain trout——the biggest (I'm sorry) I had ever seen.

I nearly dropped the rod. Talk about beginner's luck; this was fantastic! The fish splashed and fought, and I thought surely I would lose it. But I managed to bring it in and get it into the basket, praying through the whole thing.

Still shaking a bit, I again worked out the line and laid it out over the water as far as I could. This time a trout took the fly before it even hit the water! I was even more excited than before. Two trout in two tries! This was unbelievable. I knew who was responsible and thanked Him, for it would have been more my speed to have spent my whole vacation fishing and never gotten a bite . . . .

"But Master, we've been fishing all night, and we haven't caught anything." Christ looked at Peter and said quietly, "Put your net over on the other side of the boat." Peter was on the point of asking what earthly difference that could make, but Christ cut him off with a nod. Shaking his head, Peter obediently lowered the net——and got the greatest catch of his life . . . .

The third time it happened, I was laughing so hard I couldn't talk. The fourth, the fifth, and the sixth were like a favorite daydream, run over and over. On the seventh, I began to admire the full sweeping curves I was getting with the line, and the fly came back alone. Thank You, Lord, for rewarding my pride. The eighth was successful, and the ninth and the tenth, and then I couldn't resist looking around to see if my family was appreciating my expertise, and once again I drew in an empty hook.

After I had caught fourteen fish in sixteen tries, Walt came up and gently took the rod from me. "You've caught two fish for each one of us," he said simply, "and that's all we could possibly eat." And I was ashamed of being the least bit disappointed at having to stop.

As he disassembled the rod and carefully placed it back in its box, Walt said, "This may be the best fishing spot in the world. There are very few people who have ever had the pleasure of fishing here, and I've never brought a party here but what we caught all we could eat." He put the box in his saddle bag, attached the basket securely to one of the pack animals, and we walked back to our base camp.

On the way back, I wondered to myself about how the trout would stay fresh till morning. The crisp mountain air was cool, but it wasn't that cool. But again, I needn't have concerned myself; no sooner did we get back than Walt simply dug a hole in the snowbank behind our tents and stuck them in.

That night, as we sat around the campfire, we were not nearly as tired as the night before. We just basked in the glow of the glorious vacation God was giving us. We shared with Walt the life in Him that we had been learning—how to praise Him in everything, and how beautifully we were blessed whenever we did. We spoke of Lee, and I told him that it was the Lord's will for her to be healed and made completely whole, and she *would* be healed, though whether He would do this on our side of the veil or on His was not for man to know.

Walt then joined with me in prayer, that the Lord would hold his wife in the hollow of His hand, and he thanked the Lord for Lee and for all the love she had given him during the years he had been so rough and ornery. He confessed to having laughed at her for her persistent faith and asked forgiveness for all the times he had hurt her. And then he looked up and grinned. "I can't wait to get back and tell her what's happened! And about this peace and——rightness——I feel just welling up inside of me. Sometimes it's so strong, I feel like shouting or something."

"Well, when that happens, go ahead and shout, Walt," I chuckled. "Up here, the worst that can happen you might frighten your horse a bit. 'Hallelujah' is what we usually say. That's just a short form of praise to the Lord." He nodded, and I thought I detected a mischievous twinkle in his eye.

We slept even more soundly that night, almost in suspended animation like bears in their winter caves. Deep in the well of sleep, I suddenly heard a tremendous *Hallelujah!*, so loud that the echo reverberated through the mountains around us. "Mary, do you suppose it's time to get up?" And she giggled. "Or is Walt just having his morning devotions?" And she laughed aloud.

In no time we were dressed. Still shivering a bit, we warmed our hands at the morning fire, and looked down into two frying pans sizzling with filets of mountain trout. I did not believe it was possible to be hungrier than we had been the previous morning, but we were. Eggs and biscuits and coffee, and then pan-fried trout——thank you, Jesus!

That morning we were able to help with the breaking of camp and the rounding up of the horses. While we were unhobbling them to lead them back to camp, a young moose strolled up, wondered what we were doing in his territory, and ambled past as if we didn't exist.

We took a last look around this beautiful grass-covered plateau and drew in a deep breath. The air was intoxicating; it made your love expand to the point where all you wanted to do was praise the Lord with every breath. We really didn't look forward to going back down to civilization, man's world, now that we had had a real taste of God's world. "Mount up," came the cry, and sure enough, not only was it easier getting up, but we had little soreness. We started down the mountain, back to Walt's ranch. This time Mary was not at all frightened. Leaning back in the saddle with one hand on the pommel, she looked as if she'd been riding all her life.

The horses were moving more briskly, now that they were headed home, and there was more conversation back and forth along the line. Also the scenery was more spectacular. Going up, our view had pretty much been limited to the back of the horse and rider in front of us and the next rise. But going down, we could see way down in the valley or for miles and miles out to the far horizon. And looking back from time to time at the hills behind us, we had a real sense of nostalgia. We wanted to go back and experience again the unspeakable delights that the Lord had created for His children to enjoy.

Up ahead Walt pointed down the trail and shook his

head. Too soon we were in the middle of what he had seen, a veritable cloud bank of mosquitoes. They swarmed so thick that they covered every square inch of exposed skin. Apparently the oxygen content of the air was too thin to permit them to go any higher, but there they waited, and the only way down was through them.

Slapping and swatting and going as quickly as we dared, down we went, but they stayed with us all the way to the ranch. As we ran inside the house, we learned that this was the first day of the mosquito season. As soon as we got inside, Walt told Lee what had happened. She could hardly contain herself with joy and weeping. She thanked the Lord for granting the prayer of her heart, and now she knew that she had a husband that was going to be with her, regardless of the Lord's will for her.

It was a blessing to be relieved of most of the tiredness of the previous two days, for the meeting that night, in the large ranch home of one of Lee's friends, was crowded beyond all expectation. Even the open stairway was covered with people, and sure enough there was Walt on the third step up.

I shared that evening about the simple Good News of the Gospel, how Jesus had come in the world that all men might have the joy of knowing for certain that they had eternal life, and that they didn't have to struggle and work and strive to be good enough. Instead, by simple faith in Christ, they could receive this priceless gift.

They listened as if they had never heard it before—possibly many of them hadn't. Then I was led to tell them of the Comforter who came to take Jesus's place, and how Jesus urged us to receive the baptism in the Holy Spirit, just as did His mother and His closest followers and all the others who were waiting in that upper room on the Day of Pentecost. I told them that the Lord intended them to have the indwelling fullness of the Holy Spirit, to enable and empower them to actually *live* the life He had called them to, for it was a demanding call. Dying out to self and surrendering one's will to the Lord totally and unconditionally was not easy; it *needed* the supernatural help of the Holy Spirit.

I told them that His gifts, every one of them, including a new language, the healing of the body and the healing of the soul, were still operating, and that God was pouring out His Spirit upon *all* flesh, all over the world, in an unprecedented revival. It was, in fact, the beginning of the greatest spiritual revolution that the world had ever known. I glanced over at Walt, who was drinking in the living word, just as I had drunk of the running water he had led me to in the mountains. He was weeping and when I asked who would like to receive the Holy Spirit, his was the first hand up.

Many people, old and young, accepted Christ as Savior that night, and many others, who already knew and loved Him but had not understood the full blessing of the Spirit, came into it. We made many good friends, but I was saddened that the man who owned that home had sat in the back, never responding, never showing any interest. The next day his wife confessed her despair to me; after we'd left he had tried to dissect the whole meeting, and she didn't see how with such an intellectual approach he would ever grasp the simple fact of Jesus as his Savior.

I mention this because in just the past few months I have received three letters from her, telling how her husband had finally received Christ in the meetings that they continued with after we'd left, and then the baptism in the Holy Spirit. He had then taken up his guitar which he had not used since he was young, the Holy Spirit had given him songs, and now he is a highlight of their growing prayer group.

The next day, we began to feel that God had completed the work He brought us there for. We had a little time of fellowship with Lee and Walt, and marveled at how quickly and deeply the Lord was moving in Walt. Every once in a while a coarse word would come into his conversation. But instead of being embarrassed and making a constrained or artificial attempt to speak well in front of us, he would simply stop and start over again and say what he meant in a different way. He knew that all he needed to do was give the Lord permission to clean him out inside, and it wouldn't be long before the words would simply be gone. This indicated that, whatever else Walt had received, the Lord had imbued him with the least-sought and most badly needed of all spiritual gifts: the gift of wisdom.

Leaving Jackson Hole was almost a repeat of leaving Ambia; people drove over to say goodbye, and there were many tears on both sides and hopes for our soon return. Best of all was their new-found determination to spread the Good News throughout their area, and this, according to the letters I receive, they have indeed done.

Once again, we waved goodbye and pointed the prow of our wagon towards California. Early one morning enroute, I got a strong urge to call the Corns.

"Walt, it's Merlin. I don't know why I'm calling exactly, except that it seemed the Lord really wanted me to."

There was silence on the other end of the phone. "Lee died yesterday, Merlin," Walt said quietly. "Her funeral is tomorrow."

"How are *you* doing, Walt?"

There was another pause, then, "Well, I can praise the Lord, Merlin, and I do. For sending you in time to tell me about Christ in a way that I could accept. For giving Lee the joy of knowing that I would follow after her. When she realized she was going," his voice broke, and he waited a moment, "all she could do was thank the Lord for granting her deepest wish. She had pain, but she died with His praise on her lips."

4. The Beginnings of a Ministry

None of us had really grasped the vastness of America, the sheer expanse of it, until it unfolded day after day in front of us. The rolling green hills and farmlands, the mighty rivers, the endless plains, the deserts, the soaring mountains—the more we saw of what God had carved and fashioned and molded, the more grateful—and worshipful, in a quiet way—we became. It was as if He were taking us through an open-air cathedral and drawing our attention to different works of art He had made to delight the eyes and hearts of His children.

We reached California on the 19th day of our vacation. The moment we did, it seemed that all we could think of or talk about was Escondido, and what our new home would be like. Finally I said, "Mary, this is silly. Here we are, dutifully sight-seeing, determined to use every day of our vacation, and all we really want to do is get to Escondido. The wagon-master is making a decision: we are altering course right now, and heading for Escondido by the most direct route I can figure out." Cheers filled the station-wagon.

And so, to Vernon's surprise and delight, we suddenly showed up one day, a week earlier than expected. Everything we saw in Escondido was even more breathtaking than Mary and I had remembered it. Our hearts were bursting with joy and anticipation, for although it was not at all the way man in his own righteousness would have done it, I sensed that God was going to do something very special—and very soon.

That acute awareness was, I know now, a special gift from the Lord, for it quickly began to fade as I became distracted by the pressing facts of our immediate needs. First of all, we had no place to live. When I had written Vernon, I'd told him that all we would need for the present was a place to park our trailer. No trailer. No problem, said Vernon. He called Wilbur Robbins and his wife, faithful supporters of the Thursday evening 120 Fellowship and they very graciously invited us to stay in their home till the Lord made clear His plan for us. And sure enough, in about a week, the Lord made a home in downtown Escondido available for us to rent.

The next concern that burdened me was the existing condition of the congregation to which we were to minister. It was one thing to come on a five-day mission, as we had three months before, and because of a tremendous amount of diligent preparation, face overflowing audiences every night. It was quite another thing to count exactly 25 people at my first Sunday service at Del Dios Junior High School. I praised the Lord, but I also confess that afterwards I indulged in a bit of serious doubting. For twenty years the Army had taken care of me completely, and for my one year as a Methodist pastor, I had started with a salary, a home, a church, and a built-in congregation.

Now, having burned all my bridges, I had a handful of people to begin a work with, no salary, and no assurance that there would be any salary; in fact, there was no promise of anything whatever. "Lord," I blurted out, as soon as I was alone, "forgive my unbelief. I know You brought us here, and I know that You're going to use us for a work, but—"

Son, how many people were in the pews, your first Sunday in Ambia?

I thought a moment. "Twenty-five," I responded sheepishly.

And how many came to your revival five months later?

"More than a thousand, Father."

And how big is Ambia?

"Father, I'm sorry. Please forgive me." I wept as I felt His forgiveness and His grace.

From that time on, I did my best to stand against such negative thinking. But overcoming is never easy, and whenever I was invited up to Melodyland Christian Center, to speak to 4,000 people, and whenever I stopped to think that there were some eight million people within driving distance, there would be a tremendous temptation to imagine what it would be like to step into a ready work like that.

But when such temptation is at hand, God always provides an escape. Quite often that is just plain old-fashioned praise. "Thank You, Lord, that I need to have my pride dealt with and my faith built up. And thank You, too, that some of Your mightiest oaks start from the tiniest acorns. Hallelujah, You're in charge, and that's all that matters!"

But if my faith faltered, Vernon's never flagged for an instant. He *knew* that God was going to raise up a major work in Escondido; he knew it so strongly I almost felt sorry for God if He didn't. And it did help to hear him describe in glowing detail all God was going to do.

It only took two services, the Thursday night meeting of the 120 Fellowship in the old Women's Club, and that unforgettable first Sunday at Del Dios, for the Lord to start sending new people to us from every direction. Once again, they were exactly the opposite of what a new pastor, in the natural, might hope for. Instead of being wealthy, healthy and with no great problems, it seemed that every single newcomer came in to us in a state of financial disaster. And talk about problems! These people had some of the most incredible problems I'd ever run across. They needed massive amounts of prayer and counseling. I smiled to recall how foolish I'd been to think that the human misery existed only in slums. And though I could not see it at all then, God was carefully hand-picking each one of these people to play a crucial role in the work He was about to undertake.

During this time I was continuing to travel to other parts of the United States, spreading the message of praise. There was a quick trip to the Christian Booksellers' Association annual convention in Cincinnati, to launch my third book, *Answers to Praise,* which would soon join the other two on the Christian bestseller lists. There were Full Gospel conventions and churches, and one moment I particularly remember was a New Year's Eve Youth Rally in Carnegie Hall in New York, at which thousands of young people danced for joy in the aisles. They were filled with the powerful new wine of the Holy Spirit, happier than the revelers at Times Square a few blocks away, and destined to be happier by far when they awoke the following morning.

At the second Sunday, there was unabashed jubilation. Present were *50* worshippers! We were on our way. I was still tempted to implement every program I had ever learned for attracting new people, from house-to-house canvassing and letter-writing to massive publicity campaigns, but each time I was on the verge of making such a suggestion, the Lord would speak to me: *No, son. Let Me do it My way.*

Nor did God permit any structuring to enter the worship of the body of believers that we now rather grandly referred to as the North County Christian Center. We had no bulletins and no programs. We arrived only with joy in our hearts and, with a sense of expectancy, we waited to see where the Holy Spirit would lead. The services would usually begin with choruses and handclapping, our arms lifting in praise to the Lord. But we never knew for sure when the time for praise would come, or when the sermon would be given, if at all. There was no organization, no chance for man to wrest control from God. But there was invariably a smooth flow to the worship, whichever way it went, a gentle, blending harmony that could only come from the Spirit Himself.

In the next few weeks, I would continue to get suggestions that we institute this or that organized procedure, often ideas that had been in practice in the churches where our people had come from. Each time the leading I had from the Lord was no. He would evolve whatever minimal organization we needed in the fullness of His time, and in a manner uniquely tailored for us.

Too many organized services have nothing of the joy and freedom that ideally should characterize worship. Small wonder that the people who regularly attend them have frequently expressed concern over the possible drudgery of Heaven. "Do I really want to go to a place where all they do is sit around for eternity singing musty old hymns?"

Worship is supposed to be as close to a prelude to Heaven as possible, but God has not designed us for boredom; He does not expect us to yearn to go somewhere for eternity that would not make us eternally joyful. On, the contrary, God has designed an eternity that will be filled with so much joy that your present body would not be able to bear being in its presence.

Yet many services do not give even a glimmer of what's in store. Their pastors have been forced by tradition, or a sense of Spiritless public decorum or solemnity into orchestrating their services for maximum "dignity" and "reverence." Similarly, their congregations have been so conditioned that if their services were suddenly to become joyful, they would think the pastor had become a religious fanatic. "The service was positively indecent this morning. Imagine, people *laughing* in God's House!"

But worship in its purest form would bring us into the presence of God in a way that our very countenances would be changed. We would glow with a radiance that the unbeliever could literally see. Joy would overcome these frail human frames, and we would lie prostrate at His feet. Praise would pour forth straight from our hearts as time passed unnoticed, and we would be swept up into realms of heavenly worship that we have never dreamed of.

It seems doubtful that we'll ever find such purity of worship on earth. But in many congregations where there is freedom for the Spirit to move as He pleases, men and women are reaching in this direction, are getting just a taste of what it could be like, and are thirsting for more. And the result is joy—*abiding* joy, not just in the service but infused into their daily life.

What kind of people are these who are filled with Christ's joy? How do they actually live in everyday situations? First, look at the life of Jesus Himself, and those who learned at His feet. Jesus was about to be crucified. He gathered His disciples for one last meal together. In these moments just a few hours before His death, He said, "These things have I spoken unto you, that my joy may be in you, and that your joy may be made full" (John 15:11, TLB).

Then, when Jesus had been cruelly and violently put to death, it was written of the 'mourners' that they ate their meals "with gladness of heart, praising God." And later, when they were in more difficult circumstances, they spent their time singing, whether in the Colosseum or in prison. For it was of such times as these that Paul wrote, "Rejoice in the Lord always, again I say rejoice."

How could they rejoice? How could Paul and Silas sing all night in the darkness of their prison cell? Because Christ's joy was theirs! His promise was fulfilled in them. His joy was not something to be enjoyed in a church service and then forgotten when life brought a crushing tragedy. That would make tragedy more powerful than joy, and Jesus came to bring victory over Hell itself. When Jesus took the horror of the Cross and made it a victory, He provided the same victory for your problems, no matter how large or ominous they might loom.

Thus, His joy is a power that causes us to face each new day with expectation rather than fear. Situations that once were hopeless are now only opportunities for God to release His strength. Believe that —really know it in your heart—and an amazing strength will begin to flow within you.

It's even scriptural! "The joy of the Lord is your strength" (Neh. 8:10). Strength locked within joy—enough strength to supply your needs a million times over. And what a way to have your needs supplied! When the Levites in the book of Nehemiah first heard these words about joy and realized what a mighty truth had been revealed to them, they all "went their way to eat, and to drink, and to make great mirth, because they understood the words that were declared unto them."

Understanding the strength that will be yours through joy will cause mirth in you, too! For joy——being spontaneous, unpredictable and explosive——has that effect. At unexpected moments, when I am not even thinking of the Lord, and unaware of the Holy Spirit's presence, suddenly a wave of intoxicating joy will overwhelm me.

This truth really came alive for me one day when Mary and I drove to the Pacific coast, left our shoes and socks in the car, and went for a long walk on the beach. It was a glorious, warm, hazy-sunny afternoon, with a few wisps of clouds in the sky and the ocean so calm that the waves hardly made a sound.

There was no trick to feeling joyful then, walking through the edge of the waves' run-out, and in my joy I thought, Oh, God, there are so many of Your people in the world who don't know this joy, who haven't learned to really love You or receive Your love. I wish there was something I could do—

When they are filled with joy, it will reach down to their feet.

To their feet, Lord?

Yes, to their feet.

I'm sorry, I don't understand.

When My joy reaches their feet, they will be able to dance before Me in praise.

Then, Lord, I should be able to dance before You right now, if that's what You want.

Yes, dance as a little child in joy before Me.

To Mary's surprise, I suddenly hopped on one foot twice, then on the other. Back and forth I hopped and opened my mouth to laugh out loud. But instead of laughter, out came a song—the first the Holy Spirit had ever given me: "My feet have got the message. They're filled with joy and praise."

It wasn't much of a song, but the words came forth over and over, and that cheerful little refrain has been used by God to bless many people. I have stepped into churches where joy has seldom if ever been experienced, taught them the song, and then encouraged them to hop a little.

Initially, the reaction would often be one of confusion and consternation. "What in heaven's name is he trying to do?" But as a few were willing to respond in obedience, the others caught on, and before long they all would be laughing. They might be self-conscious, but they couldn't help smiling. The seed was sown. After such sessions literally thousands of people have come up to me and said, "You know, that's the first time I've ever really enjoyed coming to church."

Such was the sheer power of joy, and it was one of the reasons why we were led not to structure our own services. We wanted the Holy Spirit to be in charge, free to introduce joy into our worship, when and how He chose.

As for the building up of the body of believers, we wanted that to be His, too, not ours, and so none of the 'tried and proven' schemes that were suggested were ever implemented. No, God was to have a free hand to do it His way, and the way He chose to do it was both time-honored and scriptural. It was also totally beyond the power of man to influence, one way or the other. He had used it many times before, to bring people to a new work or introduce a new ministry; in fact, He had used it to first bring people to hear the teaching of His son.

5. A Ministry of Healing

Healing was a regular part of our service, though as I've said, there was no telling from one Sunday to the next which part of the service it would be. One Sunday in the early fall of 1972, I was strongly led to open right off with a time of prayer for healing. I'd never done this at the beginning of a service, but there was no questioning the strong guidance I was receiving that morning.

We had already had a number of dramatic healings in our services, and word was beginning to spread that God was doing something pretty unusual at the North County Christian Center. This kind of news has a natural attraction for anyone with a physical infirmity, and on this particular morning a certain family arrived to see what exactly was going on at Del Dios Junior High.

They came with an attitude of understandable doubt, but also with a great need and a willingness to believe. The mother of the family had a severe heart ailment which had required years of careful attention and heavy medication—so heavy that it amounted to 27 different pills a day. And this was just to keep her heart functioning well enough and her blood thin enough to enable her to do even minimal work around the home.

I invited those who wanted to be prayed for to come forward and asked those members of the body who were so led to stand behind them and join with me in prayer. The mother on medication came and stood before me. Together with the brethren around her, I asked God to touch her blood stream and her weakened heart and to bring healing into her body.

From all outward appearances her faith did not seem to be very strong, but she was surrounded by the Lord's people who were believing with her for His healing touch. It has often been my experience in such cases that, while an individual's own faith may not be very great, the Lord can supply others who will believe with them, and provide additional channels through which the Holy Spirit may do His work.

In this situation the Holy Spirit was able to bring her to such a state of faith and confidence that God healed her. When it happened, her face lit up with joy and praise, and she testified then and there that she had been healed and knew it. The whole congregation as one joyously gave thanks.

Whenever someone is healed in church, I ask them to go to their doctor and get confirmation from him of what the Lord has done. Often a doctor will not commit himself, and use terms like 'mis-diagnosis' or 'spontaneous remission', but many are willing to attribute the recovery to God's healing power. In this particular case, we could not, of course, advise her to stop her medication until she was released by her doctor. As it turned out, this medication provided additional confirmation of an undesired sort. The woman was not able to see her doctor for two days and in the meantime the medication caused her to bleed profusely.

When the doctor examined her blood he discovered that it was now much too thin, made so by the continuing medication. He took her off the medication, immediately put her under observation, and shortly discovered that somehow this woman's heart had been completely renewed and her blood had become perfectly normal.

Word began to spread as far as San Diego, an hour away, and we started to have healing services every Sunday evening. To one came a young Presbyterian in a cast that ran from his foot clear to his hip. He was not there of his own volition, but only to please his parents, who had begged him to come. The broken bones in his leg would not knit together properly, and an attempt by his doctors to alleviate the condition had failed. He made no secret about the fact that he was there under protest, and when several people stood and gave public testimony to the healing that God had brought them, this young man made it clear to all within earshot that he did *not* believe that God healed people in this modern day and age.

At the close of the service, I again did something which we had never done before. I invited anyone who had any kind of physical infirmity that they wanted prayer for, to come and sit in a chair beside the pulpit, in plain view of everyone, and ask the Lord to heal them right then and there.

My request was greeted with silence, and no one responded. I just waited, because I was reasonably sure I had heard the Lord correctly. Then, just when the congregation began to get restless, a tall, very attractive lady who had worked as a model came forward. She admitted that she had been reluctant but had felt such an urging that now she was confident He was going to heal her. Her problem, it turned out, was that one of her legs was shorter than the other. This was causing her increasing pain, because the difference was growing more pronounced.

Well, of all physical healings in which enthusiasm on the part of the healer could be mistaken for a genuine work of God, the worst offender was leg-lengthening. It seemed as if almost anyone sitting down in a chair and holding their legs out straight had a slight but discernible differentiation. And the enthusiastic healer, grabbing ahold of the legs and praying mightily (and maybe pulling a little) would invariably produce a miracle. I do not mean to speak disrespectfully of the works of God; I personally know of several cases where measurable differences have been equalized miraculously and permanently. I am just saying that I have also known this particular ministry to have been abused.

Perhaps for this reason, I was led not to touch this lady at all, or even get near her. She sat in the chair and extended her legs, and the difference in them was so marked that everyone present could plainly see it. I invited one of the older members of the body to come forward and pray with me, and together we united in prayer with the rest of the congregation, asking the Lord to bring His healing power upon this, His child.

Every eye was glued on her feet, and as we prayed, the shorter one began to grow. It grew even with the longer one——and kept on growing, till it was noticeably longer than the first one. The member I'd asked to assist me became a bit rattled at this development. "What do we do now, Pastor?" But I just smiled and said, "Why, we just pray that the other leg will now grow to match this one." God was in charge, and He knew what He was doing. We prayed again, and as everyone watched, the other leg grew and became a perfect match. Thank you, Jesus!

As the woman went back to her seat, praising God with all the rest of us, she was almost knocked over by the young Presbyterian, on his feet now and hobbling to the front as fast as his crutches could carry him. There was a flight of ten steps leading up to the platform where the pulpit and the chair were, and not saying anything to anyone, he resolutely and with great difficulty hoisted himself up them and sat down in the chair. After he had blurted out his problem, we prayed and asked Jesus to touch the leg that would not mend.

As we prayed, he told us later, all the doubts he had simply vanished, and he felt a strange power flowing through his body. He knew that God had done something to him. He stood up, and when one of the men held out his crutches to him, he motioned them away. Slowly, for he had trouble balancing with the heavy cast, he made his way down the steps and then hurried to the arms of his overjoyed parents.

The next day he went to his physician and asked that the cast be taken off and the leg x-rayed. The physician argued that it hadn't been on nearly long enough to accomplish anything, and that removing it now might upset any healing that was in process. But the young man insisted. The x-ray showed no break whatever, and the physician was dumbfounded.

I have never ceased to be thrilled when God chooses to mend bones instantaneously, or repair hearts or any of the other wondrous things by which He let it be known that His sovereign hand was upon a little body of believers known as the North County Christian Center. But for all the physical healings that had taken place, the deep healings of the spirit that occurred had in many ways an even more profound effect.

For years I had sought an answer as to why everyone who was prayed for wasn't healed. I had known that there had to be a good reason, but it had eluded my most careful search. Then one afternoon, as I sat at my desk looking out over the San Pasqual valley, the answer came. *My people are not healed, because they ask to be healed of the wrong thing.*

Lord?

They ask to be healed of their sufferings and what is hurting them. They should first pray to be healed of the things within them that are hurting others.

I nearly exploded with joy! God had just opened a truth to me that I knew would bring healing to many who had previously found no solution to their dilemma. And as I have been able to encourage God's children to fix their attention on this matter, they have indeed experienced wonderful healing!

Jesus taught us that the two things God wanted most was for us to love Him with all our beings, and love others to the same degree that we love ourselves. And this was the secret: pray to be healed of everything within you that is bringing pain to others, and you will experience a new and glorious relationship with the Son.

The first thing is to pray to see the ways that you hurt others, for the ways we do this are as numerous as the sands of the sea. And I don't mean just the obvious ways, such as slander or gossip. One must be sensitive to the indirect ways—the hidden jealousy or judgment or vindictiveness. For while we may not always speak what we think or feel, if we carry it in our hearts, it does damage—to ourselves as well as to others. Did you ever stop to think that arthritis may be caused by a lifetime of unspoken re sentment? That despair is merely anger with no place to go?

The physical body can often be healed while the spiritual body is left untouched in anxiety and fear. But as the spirit is healed and brought into the light, faith grows, and the individual is then free for healing in every area of his life. The Lord sent us people who were broken in spirit, worn out from bearing their own burdens and trying to be good enough to deserve God's blessing. How many people came to realize that God loved them exactly as they were and that they could trust in Christ for the complete forgiveness of all their sins and failures, I cannot say. But the word also got around that not only were people receiving amazing physical healings, but whole lives were being transformed at the very core of their beings.

We no longer had to worry about attendance at our services. Less then four months after we had begun, between 400 and 500 people were present every Sunday morning, and Del Dios was fairly bulging at the seams.

With this sudden increase came an urgent need for rapid training and maturing of the body. Now the Lord began to point out the steps that had to be taken. The first and most obvious was for assistance in the responsibility of leadership. Once again, there were many forms of committees, boards, organizational procedures in use elsewhere that we could have adopted, but I sensed that God intended something else, something exactly fitted both to our present needs and the direction in which He planned to take us. Searching scripture, I became convinced that He wanted us to have elders with the same function and capacity as He had established in the early church.

I was well aware of how crucial a step this was and I was determined to wait upon Him until He impressed upon me the names of those He would have so appointed. I had to be absolutely certain that I was not picking them myself, out of any fondness for them or because to my way of thinking, they were the most qualified for the job. The Lord gave me five names. When I was sure that they were each one from Him and not me, I announced them to the congregation. They were overjoyed, not only to have leaders to turn to with their problems, but because, as many told me later, they all witnessed to the Lord's hand in the selection.

The next immediate need was Sunday School classes for the children. These were set up in the classrooms of the school. They did not follow any prescribed or traditional church program, but used the Bible to provide the central themes in each class. Each teacher was responsible for being sure that each child was brought quickly and surely into an understanding of what it meant to know Jesus Christ as personal Savior.

But these classes created additional administrative problems. We had to staff them, supervise the teaching, and make certain that the classrooms were left in perfect order, for, according to our agreement with the school board, we had to leave the building in immaculate condition when we left. This meant that Pastor Gortner, one of the elders or I would have to check each of the classrooms after Sunday

School to make sure that they were in even better condition than before we had used them.

For several months this system worked without a flaw. Then, one wet Sunday in February, one of the volunteers got sick and couldn't take her class. She was able to get a substitute, but neglected to mention the need for care in cleaning up the room after its use. And that particular Sunday, for reasons known only to the Lord, no one showed up afterwards to double-check.

When the home-room teacher arrived the following morning, she found some chalk on her desk, some papers on the floor, and the entire room in some disarray. She promptly called the school superintendent to complain. He in turn called the school board member responsible for maintenance, and we shortly received a letter advising us that if any classroom was ever again left in such condition, we could no longer use the school premises for worship.

The prospect of 500 people arriving one Sunday morning to find the school locked up tight and no place to worship, not even an outdoor facility, sent shivers down our spines. As it was, our one-year agreement with Del Dios was scheduled to expire in October, and their response in this situation was a fair indication that it might not be renewed. We started looking for another place to worship.

We looked high and low. We went to church after church, asking them if we couldn't possibly use their facilities when they were not in use. But no one wanted to have this strange group of people who believed in miracles and an experience called the baptism in the Holy Spirit. Nor were we any more successful in applying to secular institutions. In fact, everywhere we turned, doors seemed to be not just closing, but slamming in our faces.

And so, we praised the Lord—collectively and individually. And as we did, one member after another came to tell me he felt that the Lord was showing us that He intended us to build our own house. And this confirmed a leading that had begun to form in my own heart.

Once again, the Enemy tried to start up my doubt engine by pointing out that we had no money, no affluent members, and not nearly the three to five years it would take, even if we did have the necessary funds available. And then he went to work on the thing that concerned me even more, for I had seen congregations torn apart by dissension over building plans and construction; in fact, it seemed that no other church activity was quite so prone to disaster. Nevertheless, Thy will, not my will, be done, and there didn't seem to be any other alternative.

So once again I went before the Lord to ask forgiveness for my unbelief. "Well, here I am again, praising You like You've taught me to teach others, and still with these doubts that I know are from the Enemy."

Son, how many people were present last Sunday?

"More than 500, Father."

And how many did you think there might be, after that first service last summer?

"About a tenth that number, Lord," I murmured.

Son, the house I will build for My people will surpass your expectations by as much as the body I have raised up has.

"Lord, forgive me."

The next major crisis we faced was the increase in the number of people who came to us for counseling. It seemed that every person who came to us came in deep need. The front door of our home was opening and shutting so often, from dawn till long after dusk, that it would have been more efficient to install a revolving door.

We loved our people with all our hearts but visitors came and went in a never-ending stream, and our kids constantly brought their friends home at all hours. In addition to this, two and sometimes three secretaries who had volunteered their services to keep up with the thousands of letters we were now receiving were also in our home. It seemed like we were holding church services sixteen hours a day.

Finally things reached a point where late one afternoon, after counseling more than twenty people all day long, Mary locked herself in the bathroom with her Bible, to have a few minutes alone with Jesus.

She had just settled down and thanked the Lord, when there came an insistent knocking at the door. "Mary? Are you in there?" She didn't answer. "Listen, Mary, all I need is just a few minutes." With a sigh, she closed her Bible and went out to see what the trouble was.

The Lord already knew we needed a place to be alone with Him. He had been waiting for us to ask for it. We asked, and He made it clear that we were to start looking. Mary and I entered into our search with a real spirit of adventure. Somewhere out there God had just the right place for us, planned for us since before the foundation of the world, and all we had to do was find it. We had just one request; we wanted it to be truly secluded. For while the Lord had substantially eased our counseling burden by spreading the responsibility among our elders, any slack in traffic through our front door was more than made up for by strangers who, having read my books, were now arriving unannounced from all over the country and simply coming in.

We looked at many places. Friends would show us their versions of the ideal hideaway, but invariably their conception of hidden was not nearly as drastic as ours; I'm afraid they must have thought we were looking for a hermitage. Nowhere did we seem to get a clear witness that this was indeed the place that the Lord had picked out for us, and we were beginning to wonder if we had heard Him correctly.

Then one sunny day in February, a real estate agent called to tell me that he had just the place. This was hardly the first time that I had heard that, but there was something that made me anxious to see it. He picked me up, and we drove up into the foothills. Higher and higher we climbed, out of the residential district, past orange groves and avocado orchards. Then we started up a narrow mountain road. On all sides, citrus fruit and avocados abounded, filling the air with their fragrance.

We came out of an avocado orchard on top of one of the higher foothills, and stopped. Directly ahead of us, surrounded by orange and plum and lemon and lime and grapefruit trees, all so laden with fruit that their limbs drooped to the ground, was a little gray ranch house with a magnificent view in all directions. The only other house in sight was off to the right, atop another rise.

I couldn't believe it; it was like I had stepped into the middle of Eden. I had to show Mary! Back down we hurried. I got Mary, and the two of us went back up alone, finding our way with extreme difficulty. We got out and looked at each other, and we knew that this was the place the Lord had picked. Below us, the green valley stretched down to the town in the distance, and behind us, snow-capped mountains rose into the sky.

Mary and I had our first experience in walking over to an orange tree, plucking one, peeling it right there and tasting the sweetest fruit we had ever put in our mouths. But above all, the sense of peace and tranquillity that pervaded the hilltop made our hearts yearn to be there. We asked the agent what price the owner, who lived on the other rise, was asking.

Our hearts sank when we heard the figure, and we realized that we could not possibly afford it. We asked the real estate agent if there were any chance the owner might come down on his price, and he said no, the owner had plenty of money and was primarily concerned that the people who bought would be exactly the sort of neighbors he wanted.

That night Mary and I prayed together. We still sensed that the Lord intended us to have that place, and so we asked Him to tell us what amount to offer. He gave us each the witness of the identical amount, and the next morning we went to meet the owner whom we immediately liked. Then we stopped by the real estate agent's office and told him of our offer. He looked at us incredulously. "You can't be serious! Why if I tell him that, he's just going to laugh."

I suggested that he go anyway, and just tell the owner the figure the Lord had given us, and we would leave it in His hands. "All right," the agent said, "I'll go, but I'm telling you, it's just a waste of time."

About an hour later the phone rang at the house we were renting. It was the agent, and he was laughing. "I don't understand it," he said, "it doesn't make any sense at all. The owner says he likes you and Mary, he wants you to be his neighbors and to have the house—at your, or rather the Lord's price."

"Praise the Lord," I said softly. "Praise the Lord."

6. God's People—God's House

To build the Lord's house .... Vernon Gortner had been enthusiastic about the prospect from the very beginning; in fact, he had been ready to build before it even became necessary to consider doing so. Now he was ecstatic. He had admired a church that had been built in the area and had acquired their plans. He was convinced that they were exactly what the Lord would have for us.

He gave the plans to a member of our body named Ray Mann. Ray was a building contractor who had a great desire in his heart to build a house for the Lord. After going over the plans in minute detail, Ray decided that he could build the church with certain modifications. He spent many hours going over the plans to determine how they needed to be adjusted to meet our specific needs.

And now we began to see—and marvel—at the diverse skills of the people that God had called to be a part of the work that He would raise here. It turned out that among our people were expert carpenters, masons, electricians, roofers, cabinet makers, joiners, plumbers—every conceivable trade that would be needed in a major construction project such as the one we envisioned. It was as if an expert personnel administrator had summoned them from all over the country for a specific job. In a sense that is exactly what had happened. God, of course, was bringing them for the sake of their souls, not their skills, but He was also giving them an opportunity to express their thanks through the abilities He had given them.

One after another, without being asked, they came forward to volunteer their services, when and wherever they might be needed. We weighed their suggestions carefully and then requested that they begin acquiring the materials that would be needed to build the Lord's house. As for funding, the Lord had indicated that we were not initially to take out a loan of any sort. He would provide the amounts we needed as the needs arose. And so with a great deal of faith and very little capital, we proceeded to put in orders for the first materials we would need.

During this whole period, I was extensively involved in traveling throughout the United States, as well as hurrying to finish my fourth book, *Praise Works,* in time for the annual Christian Booksellers convention in Dallas that summer. Yet in the midst of all this, I was repeatedly moved by the Spirit to take another look at the plans for the church, which by this time had reached a very advanced stage.

As soon as I had an opportunity to do so, I took them home and really studied them. I could not easily envision a finished work from a schematic, but as I studied the plans I became increasingly aware of a very uneasy feeling that something was wrong—very wrong. It was nothing I could put my finger on, nothing I could point to and say, "Look, this just won't do." Because of this I had an extreme reluctance to say anything at all. I was thrilled at the enthusiasm these men were showing, and the love that was flowing through them for one another, as well as for the project. "Lord," I prayed, "these men are giving their all for this work, and doing the very best that they know how. If something's wrong, if they should stop and wait for more direction, You're going to have to help me to know what to do. Please take over. I will trust that everything will come out right."

Not long before construction was scheduled to begin, the Lord brought Randy Paul from Los Angeles to join us. Until a year and a half before, Randy had been one of the largest building contractors in southern California, involved in developing vast tracts of land and undertaking major industrial installations. He was tall, confident, good-looking, aggressive and successful——the epitome of the American ideal. By grit and ingenuity, he had built up a million dollar business of which he was extremely proud.

One morning, in the early part of 1971, Randy started off the day on top of the world and ended the day with the world on top of him—$250,000 in debt. In his rapid expansion, he had so pyramided his business ventures that the funding for each construction job depended upon the completion of the one ahead of it. His overlapping time margin for safety had grown so thin that finally one day on one construction site the work crew became disgruntled at not being paid on time and decided to walk off the job. Home they went, taking all Randy's tools with them. Another crew on another site, hearing what happened, decided to do the same, and they called their friends on a third site and so on. By noon every crew he had had walked off the job, taking their tools and his tools with them.

Word of his misfortune spread like wildfire, and in hours his creditors and subcontractors were on the phone, each demanding that he be paid immediately, before Randy settled any other debts. But unfortunately the job which would have paid all these debts and all the payrolls had not been completed, and there was no ready cash available. Then the banks had begun phoning to call in their demand loans. And Randy was wiped out.

But that was not the worst of it. When his books were audited, it turned out that Randy had not bothered to keep up withholding tax and social security benefit payments to the federal government on all his paychecks, with the result that he suddenly found that he owed the government $100,000. Immediately the government put liens on everything Randy owned. He was forbidden to work as a contractor or become involved in any kind of business until he paid the government every cent he owed.

When the State of California got wind of what the federal government had done, they, too, taxed anything that Randy owned, with the end result that Randy was forced to give up any hope of ever re-establishing himself as a businessman. His lawyers advised him to go into bankruptcy, but he was determined somehow, some day, to pay off every cent he owed, and he started by selling his home to pay all the men who had worked for him.

But Randy was a strong man and still proud, and he said, "Well, I've still got my health, and my family is well." The next day he received word that his daughter was in the hospital in Las Vegas, with suspected meningitis. Randy and his wife Kathy flew to Las Vegas and awaited the verdict of the doctors. It turned out it wasn't meningitis, but now Kathy began to crumble under the strain they had endured, the loss of their home and everything they owned, and now the severe illness of their daughter. Her nerves began to give way, and she was on the verge of a complete breakdown.

Finally, Randy's own health began to fail him, and in a few weeks he found himself on his back, unable to work, unable to help his family or himself, unable to do anything at all. Utterly helpless, for the first time in his life, he lay there, staring at the ceiling of his and Kathy's bedroom in the house they were renting, tears of frustration in his eyes. And in this broken condition his heavenly Father, whom Randy had known but had not heeded for many years, was able to get through to him.

Randy, I want you to give Me your life in service.

Randy had never had much time for the Lord. He had

been a member of a church, but it was mainly a social thing with him, the proper thing to do, and he seldom bothered to go. Now, all of a sudden, God was calling him to an accounting, to go back over his whole life and see what it all added up to. Not very much, Randy realized, when put on His scales. And there, in broken health and without even hope to cling to, Randy asked God to make something worthwhile out of his life.

In April, 1972, Randy heard about a retired Army chaplain who was coming to Los Angeles to speak. When the date of the meeting arrived, he was well enough to attend. The message of praise was new to him. It stirred something deep within him, something he had not felt in a long time: hope. If what this Carothers fellow was saying were true, he had a humdinger of an opportunity right then to praise God for everything about his present circumstances, as well as everything that had befallen him. Hope welled up within him as he heard of what had happened when other people had begun to praise God, and he knew beyond question that God had brought him to this exact moment in order to do something very special in his life.

At that moment I gave an invitation to the congregation for all who wished to trust Christ and then to receive the fullness of the Holy Spirit to come forward, and one of the first was a tall, handsome, virile-looking man, with something very distinctive about him. Randy realized then for the first time what it meant to commit his whole life to Jesus and receive the free gift of eternal life. As he described it later, when he turned all his needs over to the

Lord, it was like a great weight being lifted from his shoulders, a weight that had been there so long he was only fully aware of how heavy it had been after it was removed. And when the prayer for the fullness of the Holy Spirit was spoken, this, too, Randy received, in complete trust.

Several months later he heard that I had come to Escondido. Since he had no job nor any opportunity of getting one, he left his wife and children in their rented home in Los Angeles, came to Escondido, rented another home, went back, packed up, moved his family into it, and joined our body at North County Christian Center.

Randy was overjoyed to be a part of us, and when he learned that plans for a new church were in the final stages of preparation, he asked if he might see those plans. He had no work of his own, and this was an area in which the Lord had blessed him with a natural gift. Maybe he could be of help and at last start serving the Lord.

He was given a set of the plans and took them home to review them. No sooner did he unroll the top print than he realized that the structure would be totally inadequate, that it did not seem to fit at all the direction in which the Lord seemed to be leading, and that technically the design was shot through with misconceptions.

But he also realized that the men responsible were doing their level best for the Lord. He was still overcoming a problem with feeling superior, and he was extremely reluctant to say anything. So he continued to pray for the Lord's guidance. The Lord granted his prayer by increasing his agitation, till, in a state of great unrest, he asked to see me at my home.

"Pastor, I'm sorry for what I'm about to say. I wish I didn't have to." He paused and looked me in the eye. "I've been over the plans a dozen times, and that building they're planning is all wrong." And he waited for my reaction.

He was astonished when I said, "Randy, you're witnessing to something that the Lord has been telling me for some time, but I did not know exactly what it was that was wrong. I'm not even sure now what should be done." We agreed to continue in prayer and trust the Lord to show us exactly what He would have us do.

A few more days passed and Randy called me again, with an even stronger impression that the Lord wanted him to do something about improving the plans. I said that there was going to be a final planning session at our house the very next night, and I invited him to come and share whatever the Lord had placed on his heart. I asked him to join with me in praying particularly that no one would be offended or hurt, or would misunderstand what he was trying to say.

All the next day, Mary and I and Randy united in prayer. As the evening drew near, I cried out to the Lord to prevent any schism. I knew only too well that any man who has given everything he has to a project, is going to have a problem if somebody tells him that he's all wrong, especially if his pastor stands by in silent agreement. The Old Boy was at it again, throwing thoughts at me like, "Well, now you are going to see your good church split right down the middle." But I did my best to rebuke such thoughts and keep my eyes on Jesus. I trusted Him to be in control of the situation no matter what developed. I knew He would use it all to His glory.

Randy, I learned later, was going through a similar struggle. At one point he even decided that he simply wouldn't come to the meeting. But he knew he had no choice. About ten minutes before he was due to leave, Kathy called to him and said, "You know, you're going over there to tell them all the things that are wrong with their plan, but you don't have a single positive thing to contribute. Don't you think you ought to have at least *something?*"

How often God speaks to us through the lips of a spouse! Randy hit his forehead with the heel of his hand, rounded up some drafting paper and a pencil and sat down at the dining room table to make some hasty sketches. Something modern, low, Spanish, easy to heat and to cool, easy to service, with plenty of windows for light and air, and above all, easy to add on to. Right then he added another sketch showing sizable possible additions on either side of the sanctuary, and a second story of classrooms for Sunday School. Hastily rolling them up, he snapped a rubber band around them, threw them in the back seat of his car, and headed for the foothills.

At our house, it was a time of real testing for Mary and me. Mary decided to get the kids to bed early and spend the evening in prayer for harmony.

Promptly at 7:30, the brethren arrived——Ray Mann, Paul Barefoot, Blaine Belaiz, our roofer, Roy Bullard, and Randy. As usual, we greeted each other with hugs and praises to God, and I couldn't help noticing how excited they were. Even before the meeting began, they were sharing with one another how they had found material that no other construction job had been able to locate, how they had gotten an incredibly good price on it, and how the Lord seemed to be blessing every move they made.

Finally, we got the meeting started, had prayer and thanked the Lord for all He was doing. By this time the others were openly curious as to what Randy was doing there. I told them that Randy had a burden on his heart regarding the plans, and I had felt that it was something that needed to be shared before this group.

I could sense that Randy was very nervous. When he tried to begin, it was difficult for him to speak. He said he knew how much the Lord had been using these men, but that he felt constrained to make some suggestions. Then he asked for a set of the plans. The six of us gathered around the kitchen table while he took a pencil and began pointing out first one difficulty and then another. As he did, he grew more confident. Though he never came on from a high position, it was obvious that he knew what he was talking about.

The first major area of difficulty, he pointed out, was the style of the church itself. It was beautiful, but old-fashioned. It would be impossible to expand upon it in any direction, should the Lord ever bring many more than the 400 people it was designed to accommodate He stressed another thing that none of us had thought of: it would be extremely difficult to build using any kind of unskilled labor, and unskilled labor was going to be the one thing we would have in abundance.

As Randy spoke, I looked around the table at the others. There were no expressions of approval or disapproval, just calm interest. It was impossible to tell how all this was going down. Lord, these men are relatively new to the Spirit; are they going to be able to accept this as from You?

When Randy was through, there was silence. Then Ray Mann spoke: "Do you have something that you would like to propose?" he asked quietly.

"Thanks to my wife asking that same question just as I was about to go out the door, I do." And he got out the drawings he had sketched.

Again the men gathered around the kitchen table, while Randy pointed out the details of his quick improvisation. And again, I could not tell from their expressions what was going on inside of them. They had only just learned to praise the Lord for everything, they had never built a church before, and were not used to working together in the Spirit. And they *certainly* were not accustomed in their construction work to having everything come to a dead stop and then head in a completely different direction. And what about all the material that had already been acquired and would have to be returned, possibly at a loss? Contracts had already been let, Roy and Paul and Ray and Blaine had spent weeks of work trying to find just the right——*Son, you are not trusting Me.*

It was true; I wasn't. I realized then that it could go both ways and still be entirely under His control. Everything

93

could be resolved in harmony, and that would be His will. Or He would permit everything to blow sky high, in order to have us put all the pieces back together again and learn a deep lesson about loving one another in Christ in the very midst of conflict. The only thing that mattered was that the heart of every man in that room was turned towards the Lord, and I knew that every one was. No matter what happened, Jesus would be glorified. I'm sorry, Father. *Take another look around the table.* I did, and my heart leaped; here and there were nods of approval!

"Say, Randy," asked Blaine, rubbing his chin, "just how many people will this church of yours seat?"

"Well, initially the sanctuary will hold 800——"

"*800!*" exclaimed Paul. "Why that's twice as many as we'd planned on. But you know," he added pensively, "we've been getting well over 500, for the last four Sundays . . . "

"And if we add the additions you mentioned?" asked Ray.

"If we do," Randy said, pointing to the sketch, "we'll pick up 200 here, and 200 here, for a total of 1200."

"1200 . . . " someone said in a low voice, and we all paused as the enormity of the figure sank in. "Hallelujah!" burst out Ray, and that said it for all of us. We all joined in, and Mary came out of the back of the house to see what all the commotion was. "Well, praise the Lord!" she said, with a smile and a deep sigh.

With what amounted to a mandate from the brethren, Randy Paul went to work on the new plans. He worked night and day to get them ready as quickly as possible. When they were completed, he turned them over to Ray, and a construction target date of June 1, 1973, was established.

Everything shifted into high gear. Volunteers to work on the project were now dropping in from the sky, it seemed. So many appeared that I began to be seriously concerned as to what to do with all of them. I had visions of swarms of eager beavers descending on the site with no one there to tell them what to do, and causing endless confusion by just doing whatever they thought needed to be done. If all those years in the military had taught me anything, it was that there always needed to be one person in charge. But—*son . . .*

A short while later, Ray Mann took me aside after one of the services. "Pastor, can I speak to you for a minute?"

"Sure. What's on your mind?"

"Well, this doesn't make any sense at all, but I'm pretty sure the Lord has been telling me to give up my contracting business entirely, and devote all my time to building the new church." He smiled and shook his head. "I've got no savings to speak of; I doubt that I've even got enough set aside to meet our house payments for however long it would take, but that's what He's telling me, and so I guess that's what I'm going to do."

As it turned out, Ray didn't have enough set aside to cover his house payments. But God knew that, and each month, just as the money was due, people would come up to Ray and say, "The Lord told me to give this to you." At

95

first it dealt with his pride a little, but in the end he would just say, "Thank you, I do appreciate it, and you're an answer to prayer." Ray later confessed to moments of fear in the beginning. These gradually vanished as each month he and his wife Edna would wind up with just enough to meet their needs—never in excess but always just enough.

So now we had an ideal supervisor, and once again I realized I needn't have concerned myself. The first thing that needed to be done was to grade the site. The Lord had chosen nine acres nestled into the side of a hill four miles out of town on Route 78. The site was in fairly open country, with plenty of parking space available, and was easily accessible from freeways and cities in all directions.

And as He had and would, the Lord provided just the right man at the right time for each job that was needed. We needed someone to see to the grading, and up stepped Brooks Cavanaugh, who had worked in the city manager's office of nearby Vista, California. Brooks was an expert at grading and knew exactly the right layout for the type of building we proposed to build. He laid out the grading and then helped to prepare the necessary forms and plans that would be turned in to the county for approval to begin construction.

That brought up our next concern: county approval. Our contractors knew from experience that such approval could take as long as a year, if the building committee started requesting changes, and it was normal for them to do so. So the body at Del Dios, where our agreement was due to run out in four months, made the approval of the plans our number one prayer concern.

When the plans were submitted to the committee, their reaction was, "Fine, we'll get to them as soon as we can, almost certainly before the end of the year."

"Isn't there something you can do to speed things up?" Ray asked. "We've got an urgent mission to get the Lord's house ready as soon as possible, and we're to break ground tomorrow."

"Mister, everybody that comes in here has an urgent mission of some sort. With the backlog we've got, we can't possibly get to it before October. If then."

The following Sunday, I asked Ray to come forward and explain what had happened. Then I spoke to the congregation. "I know how disappointed you must be; we've been looking forward to getting out there and starting for so long. Well, there is nothing we can do." I paused. "Except pray. And that we should know how to do by now. But we don't, or God would have moved on that Committee's heart. Now if you *really* want to build God's house, you will really start to pray. And I mean *pray*—the first thing when you wake up in the morning, at mealtimes, when you're driving, shopping, cleaning, working, and the last thing before you go to bed at night. If we don't want to celebrate Christmas standing in the rain, we had better become prayer warriors pretty fast."

A week later, we learned that our plans had somehow been moved to the top of the building committee's agenda and approved with only a few minor alterations.

7. *Building the House of the Lord*

At 10:00 A.M. on the morning of June 1, 1973, to the accompaniment of cheers and the roar of a diesel engine, the blade of a big yellow bulldozer driven by one of our own men bit into the brown soil of our church site. We had begun to build the Lord's house!

So many unskilled people wanted to help that at first Ray was hard-pressed to find work for them, but a regular program soon evolved. A few skilled professionals and experienced amateurs donated their time during the week, and as many as half a hundred laymen of both sexes and all sizes and ages descended on the site every Saturday. In effect, it was not unlike an old-fashioned barnraising.

In fact, so much was accomplished on those Saturdays,

with people who practically had to be told which end of the hammer to hold, that it really was like a barn-raising. People driving by on Friday and again on Monday were staggered at the speed with which the shell went up. All of a sudden there was a structure on the hillside, where there had never been anything before.

Saturday would start as early as people could make it, to make maximum use of the daylight available. The Lord blessed us with ideal working conditions every single Saturday—it was always clear and sunny, with just enough of a breeze to provide cooling. By this time the Lord had spoken to Wilbur Robbins, who had recently sold his grocery business, and told him to offer his services as Ray's right-hand man. So now Ray had the help he so badly needed in just keeping all hands busy, and "What can I do now?" was no longer a question that he dreaded.

Time after time strangers would come to me and say, "Pastor Carothers, I'm a pretty good bricklayer (or carpenter or electrician), and I've just been laid off. I'd like to help you." And it would turn out that just at that time we would have a real need for another bricklayer (or carpenter or electrician), and I would praise our Personnel Director in awe.

Another source of unending joy was the sight of so many young people working side by side with their parents, glad to submit to adult authority, giving and gaining every bit as much to and from the work as their elders. We were one in the Spirit, as I had never known such oneness before. In fact, during the interim construction, when we had the shell up but the interior remained unfinished, the young people would come out to the site on their own just to sing and join hands and pray for the Lord's continuing mercy and protection on the church. And that *esprit de corps*, that spirit of the body, has remained intact ever since.

Nor do I want to slight the women-folk. They did what they could do best. Each Saturday they arrived with baskets and hampers filled with home-made pies, cakes, baked beans and potatoes, fresh-baked bread, rolls, hams, chickens, and meatloaf. The 4 × 8 plywood sheets stretched over sawhorses would sag with the weight of the abundance God had provided. And when mealtime was done — and it was always more than just a time of eating, filled as it was with rejoicing and fellowship — the women would pack away their dishes, roll up their sleeves and ask what they could do.

And so we became a body that came together on Saturdays as well as Sundays, and He showed us that He intended us to live all of our lives in closer union with one another than we had in the past.

Needless to add, we were learning new dimensions of praise, and one of them was the giving of praise: praising God for one another and commending others as the Spirit led. It's amazing what a difference a little heartfelt praise can make! I'm not talking about buttering people up; flattery is of the flesh and self-serving and does little but harm. But to be willing to be an instrument of God's encouragement, particularly when a brother or sister is in obvious need, that's a beautiful thing! And it affords the

Lord an opportunity to say, "Well done, thou good and faithful servant!"

By our being willing to praise, even when it's the last thing we feel like doing, God can lift up someone who is down and elevate them to a higher level——*and us with them.* Because, just as praising God in the most trying circumstances works a change deep within that is often miraculous, so relaying the Lord's encouragement to someone we really don't feel like commending often has an unusual effect on both sides of the relationship.

How often have I heard, "That person was utterly unbearable——until I began to praise him. At first, I could only do it in my mind. But after awhile I was able to put it into words, even though I didn't feel it very strongly. And then the most amazing thing happened: I began to believe it. And my whole attitude began to change. And that was only the half of it, because God did another miracle: the person began to change, too!" There is power in praise! It does work——on people, as well as circumstances. For it's part of God's plan, and it works exactly the opposite of criticism and faultfinding. It lifts both the giver and the receiver. And I am convinced that we've only begun to tap the tremendous reservoir of power that's there.

Certainly praise had much to do with the high quality of work and the steady progress on the construction site.

Ray was constantly amazed at how much was being accomplished by people who knew nothing about construction, but who simply had willing hearts. We had been told that it would take a full construction crew one year to complete the building, but we sensed that the Lord was going to speed things up considerably: one look around on any Saturday made that obvious. People who had never handled hammers before were discovering that there was a rhythm to nailing that made it infinitely easier. They were thrilled to find that they could drive an eight-penny nail home in four blows. But every so often they would forget to pray, and the noise of construction would be punctuated with "Ow! Praise the Lord, I did it again!"

In one month we were ready to raise the roof beams. And just when we needed him the Lord provided another man, Ed Boyer, who happened to have just the crane we needed to lift them into place. When it was time to put on the roof, it seemed like everyone wanted to get up there and participate in nailing down the roofing boards. Ray was glad to oblige them, for we were anxious to complete the roof as quickly as possible.

Another thing that astonished the professionals was how neatly little details were coming together. In the building trade there are some time-honored expressions like, "Come on, you're not building a grand piano," or "They'll never see it from the highway." For in any job there were bound to be places where seams did not quite meet or boards from the lumber yard were warped or not evenly cut. And in actual construction a variance of an eighth of an inch when extended for eighty or a hundred feet, could create a significant gap. Such things were normal and taken in stride.

But on our building there was a difference. It was a common sight on Saturdays, in the middle of all the activity, to see a crew of men suddenly stop, form a circle and bow their heads, asking the Lord to guide them in their next step, committing their particular assignment, and the whole project, to His perfect care. The results gradually became apparent.

As the work progressed more and more rapidly, I once again forgot to trust the Lord and grew concerned. I knew nothing whatever about construction and began to have visions of all this eager but amateur zeal being responsible for some key flaw. Not that it would ever get to the point that someone would lean against a wall and the whole thing would fall down, but still——I asked Randy if he would go out to the site, and give it a careful once-over.

From the moment he had submitted the plans to Ray, Randy had felt that his part was finished, and that he should not be looking over anyone's shoulder. But he was glad to put my heart at rest, and several days later he stopped by my house.

"Well?"

He shook his head, and I thought, Oh no, he's found something serious.

But he was shaking his head in wonder, not concern. "I can't understand it, Merlin. Those people don't seem to know what they're doing, but I've never seen a building come together so tight——every seam, every joint, every corner. It's uncanny!"

Sorry, Lord . . .

With the roof boards in place and the tar paper laid out,

Blaine Belaiz arrived that Saturday with equipment to heat the tar and spread it over the roof. Carrying and handling buckets of boiling hot tar was a tricky job, and Ray picked his men carefully. One of them was carrying such a bucket directly above where Ed Bailey stood on the concrete floor, next to twelve-year old Ralph Wayman. Ed later said that at that instant he got a sudden impulse to reach out his left arm and knock the boy aside, and as he did so a bucket of hot tar plummeted down and went all over Ed's arm.

Ed screamed in agony. Men from all over the site rushed to his side, laid their hands on him and prayed. Immediately the searing pain began to subside, and they sensed that the Lord had His hand on Ed's arm. As they continued to pray, peace replaced fear. They began to peel the coating of tar off his arm. As they did so, flesh came with it. And then came God's miracle: new flesh, firm and pink, formed before their eyes, till the entire arm was made perfectly whole.

Work stopped, and everyone gathered to give quiet thanks to God, both for saving the boy and healing Ed's arm. Ed was one of those once highly successful men (promotion had been his field) who had come to us bereft, with no job, no money, and no prospects for the future. At one of the first services he had attended the financial needs of the building project had been made known. The last sixteen dollars Ed had to his name were in his pocket, and the Lord told him to give it. "Lord, that's all I've got." *Give it, and I will bless you.* So he did. (Today, Ed is the director of his own small but growing airline, possibly the first one entirely staffed by Christians and committed totally to the Lord.)

The fund-raising in itself was a miracle. Like all the others it was uniquely suited to our situation and in keeping with the emerging spirit of the North County Christian Center. God used the generosity of people like Ed Bailey, who had little or no means, to move the hearts of those who did have some resources. A person would give his last dollar and later share how God had blessed him, and another, hearing his testimony, would give ten. This pers n, in turn, would later testify to God's blessing, adding that it had been the testimony of the first one-dollar contributor which had inspired him, and someone else would thus be led to give a hundred dollars, rejoicing that that was the first time in their lives he had ever given so much to anything.

And so, without any exhortation, the Holy Spirit began to move. The first person to withdraw a thousand dollars from his life savings was Roy Wyman, Ralph's father, who was eventually to become an elder, a close friend and administrative assistant. And the Lord used his gift to stir others.

An unusual procedure for bill-paying came about this way: each time a bill came due and we didn't have sufficient funds to cover it (which was usually the case), we simply announced the amount that was needed and let it go at that. The Lord was showing us that here was one more area in which He would have us trust Him, no matter what. I was learning along with the rest.

One Sunday morning, I looked at the figure we had to have by the next morning, and I could not bring myself to mention it aloud. It was $10,000. "We've got another bill due tomorrow morning," I said, and there was general laughter. "It's much larger than any we've had so far." The laughter died away. "This is a real opportunity to listen to the Lord, and let Him tell you what you are supposed to do. As the Lord speaks to you, I'm going to ask you to write on a piece of paper what you are going to give and bring it up here and place it on the altar. The treasurer will add them up and give me the total before I tell you what the exact amount we need is."

When the treasurer had added up the amount of the contributions, he put the total on a slip of paper on the lectern in front of me: $9,950. I was about to speak, but the Lord seemed to say *wait*. So I just stood there, and everyone in the congregation sat perfectly still. Abruptly someone got up and hurried down front "I'm supposed to give $50 this morning," he blurted out and hastily returned to his seat. With tears of joy, I announced to the congregation that the amount we needed, $10,000 had just been met, to the last dollar. Gasps went up, followed by cheers and hallelujahs.

Each step of the way, we were led to minimize our emphasis on financial needs. I had seen congregations become overtaxed by repeated exhortations to give; often people became exhausted and nearly sick of the project by the time it was finished. Yet I knew that the Lord intended our giving to be a joy, not a bondage, and we did everything in our power to keep it that way.

And so, scarcely a month and a half after we had begun, the building was up and the roof was on. Each stage of construction was a new schoolroom for the Holy Spirit to teach us to trust and obey, and to listen to Him through the lips of those around us. For most Christians, that's easier said than done. We like to get our truth directly from above. But the fact is that 95% of it is going to come from our brothers and sisters—one of the reasons why the Lord has called us into a body.

God was teaching us to trust His Spirit in one another, and listen for Him no matter what was said or how. People would come from all over with suggestions, and I would try to listen with an open mind, no matter how zany they might seem. I soon learned that some of the wildest proved to be right-on, and some of the most apparently practical proved unfeasible. In each case all I could do was listen carefully and inside pray to know if this was of the Lord or not.

A good example of this came just before the tiles were going on the roof. A man named Harold Schauer came up to me and said that our church was going to have the most magnificent cross on it that had ever been on top of any church. I said, "Oh?"

"Yes, it's going to be thirty-six feet tall, and lighted red on one side and white on the other. It will revolve and will have a descending dove circling above it!"

I tried not to wince. Why not have horns blowing and neon lights flashing and—of all the garish, carnival midway ideas! I mean, what was this guy trying to do to our church? Doesn't he—

Son, you're not listening.

You mean, *You* sent him? But Father, a circling dove—

Trust Me.

I did. What other choice did I have? We gave the go ahead, and before the cross was finished, Ed Bailey, who knew nothing of it came up to me one day in great excitement. He had, he said, just seen a vision of our church with a huge, revolving cross on it. It was magnificent, a breathtakingly beautiful gift of the Lord. And about that time I learned that Harold was one of the top sign designers on the West Coast.

Our cross has brought many passers-by inside, to see what kind of people worshipped under such a dramatic sign of the crucifixion of our Lord Jesus Christ, and more than a few have been so touched by the love and flow of fellowship that they remained to become a permanent part of the North County Christian Center.

8. The Work is Finished

As any builder knows, interior decorations of a building can be immensely time-consuming. Long after the shell is up and the roof on, the work continues inside. People, looking at the outside, wonder what's taking so long. And so it was with us. We could hardly wait to get inside and start worshipping, and the pace of completion continued to surpass all expectations.

Again the Lord sent the precise people we needed when we needed them. I stood in awe of His thoroughness and timing. Sometimes we would think that He was not acting upon what seemed to be a pressing need, only to discover later that He had indeed been moving in a heart a thousand miles away, and that the need was not quite as pressing as we had imagined. It could wait until the person that God was moving upon to come arrived, and then the completion of the task would fit perfectly into the flow.

Help in co-ordinating the whole interior design was one of our most pressing needs. What kind of pews should we have? What kind of trim would go with the contemporary Spanish-mission flavor of the exterior? What color should the carpeting be? The walls? The bathrooms? These were the decisions that needed to be made and I had no knowledge of color scheme or design. I appealed to the Master Decorator, and He sent an obedient and gifted servant named JaNielle Theisan, a professional interior decorator in San Diego, who volunteered her services.

Again, it was a case of trust. JaNielle had many unusual ideas, many things that had never been done in a church before. As she confidently described color schemes as if she could already see them, I had to remind myself more than once that I had God's assurance that He had sent her, and He was in charge. The end justified the means: everything flows together as if it had been all fore-ordained, and there is an atmosphere of peace and reverence in the sanctuary that could only have come from God.

During this period, a young man by the name of Phillip Pascoe had a serious motorcycle accident in the Escondido area and wound up in the hospital. One of our young people who go there regularly to minister to the sick, visited with him and shared the Good News. Trusting in Christ as his Savior was not something that Phillip could accept on intellectual terms, but there was no mistaking the genuine joy and excitement of the person who sat next to his bed. When he was told of the new house that God was building out on Route 78, Phillip said, "I wish I could make the stained-glass windows for your church.

It turned out that while he had done no windows of his own in the States (the quality of which could have been easily checked) he had served an apprenticeship, and had worked on stained-glass windows in Europe. When he was released from the hospital, I contacted Phillip. "They tell me I'm on workmen's compensation and am not allowed to go back to work until I'm completely healed. So in the meantime I would like to do your windows for free. All you'd have to do is pay for the materials and the glass."

Was he able to do it? Did he have any real talent? Or did he just mean well? Lord—

Do not be afraid. This is of Me.

And several months later, when the windows were installed, we witnessed another miracle, this time in glorious technicolor. Though the windows were modern in design, they were also evocative of the distant past. While Phillip had no charismatic background and could not have understood their significance, the signs of the fish and the dove were woven throughout.

This happened again, as the suspended ceiling was being put in. (After much prayer, we had decided to use professionals for this extremely tricky job. The contractor told me afterwards that, in all his years of work, this was the first building he had known that was built exactly on the square.) Ed Boyer, who had assisted in designing and building the cross, now came up with a vision of a large cross of lighted panels in the ceiling of our sanctuary, with a special alternate series of lights that would enable the cross to be blood red.

A lighted cross that could be either white or blood-red? Again I wondered, and again the Lord said, *Trust Me.* The cross lights the path to the altar beautifully. During Communion we use the blood red lights which serve as an awesome reminder that it is only through the blood of Jesus that we are given the privilege of coming into the Holy of Holies to worship God.

Trust was the watchword with the carpeting that Steve Theison was led to volunteer, the sound system of speakers recessed in the ceiling throughout the sanctuary installed by Dr. Harry Beck and his son, the intricate carpentry work by Bob Koch, a retired woodworker from Canada, and the massive, four-inch-thick solid mahogany doors given by the Mel Swansons. These doors have large crosses carved in them, so that on entering the sanctuary, one goes to the Cross and through it, into the Resurrection Life. So many other gifts and talents were used in the construction of the church that it would take a whole book to describe and do justice to them.

One balmy afternoon in mid-September, I got a call from Randy, whom I'd not seen in some time. "Pastor, the Lord's been talking to me again. Can I see you right away?" I said sure, and as I waited, I thought about all that God had done recently in Randy's life.

Randy had been struggling to find his place in God's scheme of things. He felt that someday the Lord would use his talents in starting a new business, but he also knew that his old self-sufficiency had not completely died out. God in His mercy could not let him begin again until it had.

In the interim, Randy was anxious to learn as much as he could about trusting implicitly and praising God in all circumstances. At that time I was frequently trying to drive home in the early hours of the morning after late services in Los Angeles or thereabouts, and battling fatigue that was almost overpowering. When he offered to be my driver on such long trips, I praised the Lord and told Randy I'd be delighted.

Randy was a tremendous help in selling books and tapes, making arrangements and booking reservations. One night in Los Angeles, I felt a strong impulse to ask him to give his testimony. He was shocked, and prayed hard for the Holy Spirit to give him the words. He told his story briefly. In conclusion he said, "I am a businessman, not a very successful one, but I have found something that is worth far more than financial success: I have found Christ as my Savior and Lord. I have discovered a new movement in my heart that is giving me peace, and I know now what is meant by a peace which passes all understanding. I don't know what God wants to do in my life or with it, but I do know He wants to use me. I am content to wait until He shows me how."

There were 700 people there, many of them businessmen, and Randy's simple and sincere testimony struck a responsive chord in their hearts.

The long drives gave us plenty of opportunities to talk, and Randy shared the burden he was under. He still owed the government $100,000, and as long as he was forbidden to own any business or borrow any money, he was powerless ever to discharge his debts. He had taken an hourly-wage job just to bring some money in for daily expenses. But he could work at that job the rest of his life and hardly make a dent in what he owed.

The thing was, he was determined eventually to pay off every penny that he owed; he felt he owed that to the Lord. He asked Him to do a miracle and make it possible. And the Lord would minister to him: *I have a way. Trust Me, thank and praise Me that things are exactly the way they are.*

Randy obeyed. Time after time the Enemy would tell him how foolish he was, and ask him what good all that praising was doing, but Randy would only praise God all the more.

One day, a year and a half after he had begun praising the Lord, a representative from the IRS stopped in to see Randy. He wanted to know his exact financial status, what potential he had for earning a living, and what had happened during the time since the collapse of his business. Randy resisted any temptation towards bitterness, and told him all he could. The Revenue agent informed him that he would be in touch, after an evaluation had been made.

Now came a new time of praising the Lord and wondering what exactly He had in mind. Two months passed without a word. Then, just as unexpectedly, the agent came again. The government realized that there was no way Randy could ever repay the money he owed them unless he were free to go into business for himself. And since it did seem that he intended to make good on his debts, given the chance, the government was going to give him just that. If Randy would come up with $5,000, they would remove the liens for the remaining $95,000, and he would be free to go back into business again.

In the midst of his joy, Randy realized that $5,000 was more than he could find if he borrowed from everyone he knew. But the Lord had opened the door, so he knew that He must have something in mind. He continued to thank the Lord and believe that He would supply the right person. And, of course, the right person did come along and did offer to loan Randy the money he so desperately needed.

Seeing what the federal government had done, the State of California hastened to make its own offer. It was not quite as generous, but it opened the last remaining door. Randy was now free and clear to follow his desire and return to contracting. But he was not yet as dead to self as he needed to be, for the Lord continued to say, *Wait*.

Randy struggled with this, impatient, yearning to get back into the fray, yet wanting even more to be obedient. At times he would ask me if I thought now was the time, but I could not let him off the hook. "You are going to have to get your own guidance, Randy. You can hear the Lord perfectly well, and you know it."

"But what am I supposed to do now? Thank Him for the confusion of mind and indecision I feel?"

"That would be a good start."

"You're right, Pastor," he sighed. "That's where I'll start."

Finally, after Randy had reached a point where he did not have enough money to pay his grocery bills and was totally dependent upon gifts of food from people who were led of the Spirit to offer them, God gave him the clear signal that the time had come. *I will open the doors, and I will provide the resources.* From that day on, the phone started ringing. "Will you build me a home?" "When can you renovate my house?" "I have in mind a small office building, nothing too elaborate"—and the orders began to pile up. Consulting with the Lord carefully each step of the way, Randy began to build his own crew, and his capital began to grow. (Today Randy has paid off all his debts, and his business is rapidly expanding. But now it's for the Lord, not Randy Paul.)

The doorbell rang, and it was Randy. "Pastor, I don't quite know how to say this, but the Lord has been strongly impressing me that we should stop work immediately and incorporate every one of the projected extensions, the additions to the sanctuary *and* the second story to the educational building for Sunday School rooms."

Again there was all the temptation to doubt, to confuse spiritual discernment with natural logic. Was this the Enemy playing to our flesh? Did we really need all the extra space, those extra classrooms? I knew I could not hear the Lord clearly enough myself to make that kind of decision, so I put it before the people and asked them to pray for guidance. One after another, they came to me with a feeling that we should expand, and build now the full vision that God had given us. They had peace in their hearts, and so did I.

So once again the word went out to stop, shift gears, and start again. Down came the old walls, and up went new ones. In went the lights and the trim and the carpeting. And we were finished, five months from the day we began.

9. An Ongoing Ministry

On the third Sunday in October, 1973, the North County Christian Center met to worship for the first time in God's new house — and a good thing they did because the contract with Del Dios Junior High had expired the Sunday before. The previous Monday, everything inside the church was so completely upside down that it didn't look like it would be usable for a month. But prayer has a way of bringing order out of the most impossible chaos.

I sensed the Lord would have something very special in mind to mark the first Sunday in our church, and I waited on Him for weeks for a word that would feed the people and cause them to rejoice and praise Him. But nothing came. No inspiration, no fresh new insight, nothing.

"Lord, it's Saturday night. (As if He didn't know what day it was.) "Won't You give me something?"

Silence.

"Very well, I praise and thank You that I will be going to church tomorrow morning in total need, and leaning on the Holy Spirit."

Sunday morning came and I drove to church early to be alone with the Lord for a few minutes before the people started coming. As I opened the back door and stepped inside, the Lord spoke as clearly as I've ever heard Him: *Son, take off your shoes.*

"Lord?"

Take off your shoes. You're standing on holy ground.

"Yes, Lord." And I did. "Now what?"

When you stand before My people, tell them to do the same. And tell them why.

"Lord, I've never done such a thing. Will they understand?"

They will understand.

I couldn't help but wonder, in the few minutes I had left to wonder in, what the reaction would be, particularly among our guests. For as I took a look out at the congregation, every one of the 1200 seats had been taken. There had been no publicity of any sort, but our people were so proud of their new church, they must have invited everyone they knew!

It was time to go out and start the service. I had my shoes back on, and I was trembling in them, like I was just out of seminary. Thank You, Lord, that I'm so needy. It's going to be all You this morning, for sure! Praise You, Father, for this beautiful house. When it came time for me to speak, I stood for a long while looking at them. The Spirit of the Lord fell upon me, and though I tried hard not to, I wept. The first words that I was able to get out were, "Children of the Lord, the place whereon you stand is holy ground. The Lord has asked that we remove our shoes as we stand before Him." I took my own shoes off, then turned and knelt on the steps in front of the pulpit.

With that, all the people left their pews and came forward. They knelt up front and in the aisles and many tears of thanksgiving were shed. From that time on there has never been a Sunday that the entire front of the church has not at some point been filled with people coming with hungry hearts.

So now comes the time for the training and deepening and maturing of the body, and again the Lord has provided the right leaders—people like Jeff Allen, a young elder who has been trained by the Lord for many years and is now teaching others what it means to die out to self and come alive in Christ. And Lois Barefoot who has had a dozen years in teaching and is able to pass on techniques in training, in Bible Study, and in preparing the Lord's people to present the Good News of the Gospel wherever they go.

Other men are being raised up to become deacons to take care of the day-to-day functions of the church. One by one the Lord appoints them to be overseers in all that He is doing. There is growing a gradual but ever-increasing awareness among us that each member must serve Him not only in following the leadership they have been given, but in being leaders themselves and in drawing others to the wisdom and knowledge of Christ.

Not all of the teaching comes from within, by any means. The Lord has brought many well-known apostles from other areas to share what God has revealed to them or given them a burden for. Three months ago He moved on the heart of one of the most learned—and busy—Biblical scholars in the charismatic movement to offer to teach on a regular basis. Michael Esses, from Melodyland Christian Center, called me to say that the Lord had told him that he was to offer his services to the new work in Escondido. And so every Friday night Michael, a converted Jewish rabbi and the author of *Michael, Michael, Why Do You Hate Me?*, teaches two classes on the Old Testament and brings it alive as few people can.

Saturday nights have also come alive as 600 or more young people flood into North County Christian Center for their own program of evangelism, songs and praise. Dramatic deliverances from drug addiction and alcoholism are weekly occurrences. Thursdays we have a continuation of the prayer-and-praise meeting that evolved from the old 120 Fellowship, Wednesday is Christian Training Institute, and Monday and Tuesdays we strongly urge husbands and wives to stay home and have some quiet family fellowship together.

In less than two years, our number has increased more than fortyfold. The Lord has built a new house for us, and deepened our walk with Him and our trust in Him in ways we can't even begin to measure. And we know that this is still only the beginning. On Easter Sunday, the first service was broadcast in what has become a continuing series. Television is in the vision He has given us, and we are looking forward to sending teams of young people around the world to spread the message of praise and thanksgiving. But this will happen only if we continue to trust and to wait and to praise. If we run ahead of Him, if we go high on what He has done for us, if we go into the arm of flesh the least bit, He will lift the mantle of grace instantly, and we know it.

The ministry of spreading the message of praise is also growing at a fantastic rate. The Lord has given me a particular burden to take this message inside prisons. The Foundation of Praise has been established to supply prisons all over the United States and Canada with free copies of *Prison to Praise*. Now the Spanish-language edition is going to prisons in Mexico, where conditions are far worse than our very worst.

As I travel through the United States, I often ask congregations how many of them have ever given a Christian book to a man in prison, and the question often stimulates the people to realize how few of them have carried out the commission of the Lord Jesus to go into the prison and share His love. Over and over I am reminded that when we go into the prisons to visit the downcast and hopeless, we are actually going to visit Him.

It isn't easy. Overcoming the initial resistance of wardens and chaplains still requires much prayer, patience and perseverance. Sometimes God moves beautifully to make it easier. At one time the Foundation of Praise had to plead with prisons in California to take *Prison to Praise.* Most had never heard of the book and had little or no interest in cooperating. But the Lord drew our plight to the attention of Herb Ellingwood, legal secretary in the office of the Governor, and now prison authorities from all over the state are getting in touch and requesting copies of the book. With this encouragement we reached out to the governors of other states and found a welcome and great assistance in opening the doors of many prisons. Now we receive 30 to 40 book requests a day.

Other doors are being opened to the Foundation to distribute free books. The four praise books are being transcribed into Braille and are being placed on special high-speed cassettes for listening by the blind. And requests for missions to South America and Africa are beginning to come in.

Praise is reaching everywhere, and everyone is getting involved. Last spring I received a phone call from New York. "Merlin Carothers? This is Gloria Swanson. Someone has just given me a copy of *Prison to Praise,* and I love it. But I want to find out more about the Holy Spirit."

She flew out and spent three days with us, soaking up everything she could about Jesus and the Holy Spirit. When the Lord led, she knelt with me and in simple childlike faith accepted Christ as her Lord and Savior.

During the three days she was not able to understand what I meant about being filled with the Holy Spirit, but on her last day with us, at the Sunday service, she came forward along with fifty or so others, to be prayed for to receive the fullness of the Holy Spirit.

She was filled with such joy that she laughed continually, and the next day she called from a studio in Hollywood. "Merlin, these people keep asking me who I am. They can't believe I'm the same person they saw three weeks ago. All I do is laugh and tell them how wonderful Jesus has been." And three days later, she told the whole country——on a national T.V. talk show.

Recently one sunny afternoon Mary and I were sitting outside atop our little foothill, and reminiscing about all the Lord had done in our lives. It seemed impossible that less than three years had passed since that day in June of 1971, when we drove into the little town of Ambia, Indiana, to settle down to the nice quiet life of a country pastor.

Back then, six speaking invitations a week seemed like quite a lot, but lately there have been more than ten times that number. Doors are being opened that have never been opened before, with the result that I was finding myself in surroundings in which I never expected to be. But God always had a reason. For instance, not too long ago I was at a very dressy dinner party. I was sitting at my hostess's right, and the number of forks and spoons radiating out from either side of my place setting signalled that I was about to partake of more courses than I'd ever had at one sitting. The cut crystal stemware sparkled, and the tablecloth was a gleaming white, which matched the white of the hostess's evening gown.

I was a little in awe of the whole affair and sat quietly listening to the rather sophisticated small talk when a tall glass of chilled tomato juice was set before me. In an amazingly clumsy maneuver, I reached for it and managed to upset it, sending a red tide racing across the tablecloth and all down the hostess's beautiful white dinner gown.

In the stunned silence that immediately followed, my murmur of "Thank You, Lord, for my clumsiness" was clearly audible.

"What did you say?" the hostess gasped.

"I said, 'Thank You, Lord, for my clumsiness.'"

"Why ever did you say that?" she said, standing now and coping with the tomato juice as best she could with the several napkins that were offered her, including mine.

"Because He's taught me to respond in joy for whatever He permits to happen to me."

She stopped for a moment and looked at me. "I wish I could learn to do that."

"You can."

"How?"

"The real secret is in Jesus. He came to give us a peace that passes all understanding. If you're willing to accept His peace, He is willing to give you His joy."

"Look," she said hastily, "I've got to get out of this and get changed. But I've heard about your books, and I was hoping to get a chance to talk to you. I will as soon as I get back."

And so praise opened an extraordinary opportunity to share the Good News, one which is still bearing fruit. By the end of that evening the hostess invited me to stay after and talk to her and a few friends who she thought would be sincerely interested. During the ensuing discussion, she made a positive commitment of her life to Jesus as her Savior, and her influence has now spread the Gospel to hundreds of others. All of which might never have happened had I responded to the normal way, in embarrassment or anger at my stupidity.

Each trip is an adventure, and the Lord has lately been increasing my travel schedule. Not long ago, I arrived at an airport for a meeting, and one of the men asked me if I ever got so tired of traveling that I forgot where I was.

"Well, sometimes I do get awfully tired," I said laughing, "but at least I always know where I am."

Another man in the group was suddenly inspired to ask, "Merlin, where are you right now."

My mind went completely blank. Other than being in an airport, I had no idea. I looked at him, smiled, shook my head slowly and said, "Praise the Lord."

If you wish to participate in the ministry of the Foundation of Praise, write:

Foundation of Praise
Box 2085
Escondido, California 92025

Postscript: In 1981 a new board of directors at North County Christian Center contacted Merlin to tell him that Ernie had been forced out of the church by a court order. The board offered to resign and let Merlin appoint all new members if he would agree to come back as pastor of the church. Merlin declined the offer.

Other books by Merlin Carothers that you will want to read:

PRISON TO PRAISE

Merlin Carothers first book. This book has been printed in thirty-one languages and distributed in over sixty countries. Many people have reported transformed lives as a result of reading the powerful message found in this book.

POWER IN PRAISE

An in-depth study of the working and scriptural basis for the principle introduced in *Prison to Praise:* in all things give praise and thanks to God. Praising God in one's predicaments is first acknowledging that God is in control of everything, whether or not it is in His will, and that He has the power to turn all things to good. Secondly, the act of obediently praising God begins to soften our hearts and produces a right heart attitude — a prerequisite for any act of God.

ANSWERS TO PRAISE

The proof of the pudding! No sooner did the first two Praise books come out than the phone calls and letters started pouring in. Praise works! Overjoyed Christians felt compelled to share the "signs and wonders following" with the author, adding their own testimonies to the rapidly-growing record. Miracle upon miracle, from all walks of life!

PRAISE WORKS

More letters selected from an assortment of thousands illustrate the secret of *freedom through praise!* Includes a letter from Frank Foglio — (author of *Hey, God!*) — who learned the power of praise when his daughter recovered miraculously after 7 long years in the "hopeless" ward of an institution for the mentally ill. Other letters are from a nurse, a nun, an attorney, a blind girl, a chaplain, an alcoholic and many others! Praise for brain surgery, praise for prison, praise for the Lord!

BRINGING HEAVEN INTO HELL

Now Merlin Carothers goes beyond his earlier works to explore life-changing situations which others have experienced. The author shares these discoveries of God's forgiveness, a new freedom in Christ and the power of the Holy Spirit to shed light from heaven in the midst of a personal hell.

VICTORY ON PRAISE MOUNTAIN

When Merlin Carothers met with contention and dissension in his church, he learned to apply in his own life the principles he has taught to millions of others. This intensely personal account shows how genuine, spontaneous praise often leads into valleys that are direct paths to higher ground.

THE BIBLE ON PRAISE

This beautifully-printed, four-color, thirty-two page booklet features selected verses on praise from thirty-eight books of the Bible. These are Merlin's favorite verses and were personally selected by him. This booklet makes a lovely gift with a message that will bless the reader for years.

MORE POWER TO YOU

Worldwide demand for more information on power has resulted in *More Power To You* — written for persons in everyday places who need more power in their everyday lives. Though presented in simple easy-to-read language, the author had given us profound and useful insights into serious problems of modern life. This book is a beautiful key to unlock a vast storehouse of spiritual power.

Comments, inquiries and requests for speaking
engagements should be directed to
Merlin R. Carothers
Box 2518
Escondido, California 92025